GOA

A STATE STUDY GUIDE

MARIA GOLSALVES

Published by

Hawk Press
4836/24, Ansari Road, Daryaganj
New Delhi – 110 002
Phones: 91-11-23278618, 91-11-43667199
E-mail: thehawkpress@gmail.com
www.thehawkpress.com

ISBN: 978-93-88318-89-1

Preface

Goa is a state in India within the coastal region known as the Konkan, in Western India. It is bounded by Maharashtra to the north and Karnataka to the east and south, with the Arabian Sea forming its Western coast. It is India's smallest state by area and the fourth smallest by population. Goa has the highest GDP per capita among all Indian states, that is two and a half times that of the country. It was ranked the 'best placed State' by the "Eleventh Finance Commission" for its infrastructure and ranked on top for the 'best quality of life' in India by the National Commission on Population based on the 12 Indicators.

Panaji is the state's capital, while Vasco da Gama is its largest city. The historic city of Margao still exhibits the cultural influence of the Portuguese, who first landed in the early 16th century as merchants and conquered it soon thereafter. Goa is a former Portuguese province; the Portuguese overseas territory of Portuguese India existed for about 450 years until it was annexed by India in 1961.

Goa is visited by large numbers of international and domestic tourists each year for its white sand beaches, nightlife, places of worship and world heritage architecture. It has rich flora and fauna, owing to its location on the Western Ghats range, a biodiversityhotspot.

The governor's role is largely ceremonial, but plays a crucial role when it comes to deciding who should form the next government or in suspending the legislature as has happened in the recent past. After having stable governance for nearly thirty years up to 1990, Goa is now notorious for its political instability having seen fourteen governments in the span of the fifteen years between 1990 and 2005. In March 2005 the assembly was dissolved by the governor and President's Rule was declared, which suspended the legislature. A by-election in June 2005 saw the Congress coming back to power after winning three of the five seats that went to polls. The Congress party and the Bharatiya Janata Party (BJP) are the two largest parties in the state. In the assembly pole of 2007, Congress-led coalition won and started ruling the state. Other parties include the United Goans Democratic Party, the Nationalist Congress Party and the Maharashtrawadi Gomantak Party.

The Goa Legislative Assembly is the unicameral legislature of the state of Goa in Western India. It consists of 40 members. In charge of the budget, the Assembly appropriates money for social programs, agricultural development, infrastructure development, etc. It is also responsible for proposing and levying taxes.

The Governor of Goa is a nominal head and representative of the President of India in the state of Goa. The Governor is appointed by the President for a term of 5 years. Mridula Sinha became the Governor on 26 August 2014.

This is a reference book. All the matter is just compiled and edited in nature, taken from the various sources which are in public domain.

The present book examines the different dimensions of the dynamics of development of Goa in order to understand the processes and to infer policy interventions for a healthy and sustainable development.

—Editor

ABOUT THE BOOK

Goa is a state in India within the coastal region known as the Konkan, in Western India. It is bounded by Maharashtra to the north and Karnataka to the east and south, with the Arabian Sea forming its Western coast. It is India's smallest state by area and the fourth smallest by population. Goa has the highest GDP per capita among all Indian states, that is two and a half times that of the country. It was ranked the 'best placed State' by the "Eleventh Finance Commission" for its infrastructure and ranked on top for the 'best quality of life' in India by the National Commission on Population based on the 12 Indicators. The Government of Goa is the provincial government created by Constitution of India as executive, legislative and judicial authority of state of Goa. It is located in Panaji, Goa. The key political players in Goa state in Western India are the ruling Bharatiya Janata Party, Indian National Congress, Maharashtrawadi Gomantak Party and Goa Vikas Party. The present book examines the different dimensions of the dynamics of development of Goa in order to understand the processes and to infer policy interventions for a healthy and sustainable development.

Contents

1

State at a Glance

Goa is a state in India within the coastal region known as the Konkan, in Western India. It is bounded by Maharashtra to the north and Karnataka to the east and south, with the Arabian Sea forming its Western coast. It is India's smallest state by area and the fourth smallest by population. Goa has the highest GDP per capita among all Indian states, that is two and a half times that of the country. It was ranked the 'best placed State' by the "Eleventh Finance Commission" for its infrastructure and ranked on top for the 'best quality of life' in India by the National Commission on Population based on the 12 Indicators.

Panaji is the state's capital, while Vasco da Gama is its largest city. The historic city of Margao still exhibits the cultural influence of the Portuguese, who first landed in the early 16th century as merchants and conquered it soon thereafter. Goa is a former Portuguese province; the Portuguese overseas territory of Portuguese India existed for about 450 years until it was annexed by India in 1961.

Goa is visited by large numbers of international and domestic tourists each year for its white sand beaches, nightlife, places of worship and world heritage architecture. It has rich flora and fauna, owing to its location on the Western Ghats range, a biodiversityhotspot.

ETYMOLOGY

In ancient literature, Goa was known by many names, such as *Gomanchala*, *Gopakapattana*, *Gopakapattam*, *Gopakapuri*, *Govapuri*, *Govem*, and *Gomantak*. Other historical names for Goa are *Sindapur*, *Sandabur*, and *Mahassapatam*.

HISTORY OF GOA

The history of Goa dates back to prehistoric times, though the present-day state of Goa was only established as recently as 1987. In spite of being India's smallest state by area, Goa's history is both long and diverse. It shares a lot of similarities with Indian history, especially with regard to colonial influences and a multi-cultural aesthetic.

Situated on the Konkan Coast in Western India, Goa was one of the major trade centres in India. It attracted influential dynasties, seafarers, merchants, traders, monks and missionaries since its earliest known history. Throughout its history, Goa has undergone continual transformation, leaving an indelible impression on various aspects of its cultural and socio-economic development.

History

Rock cut engraving at Usgalimal.

Rock art engravings found in Goa exhibit the earliest traces of human life in India. Goa, situated within the Shimoga-Goa Greenstone Belt in the Western Ghats (an area composed of metavolcanics, iron formations and ferruginous quartzite), yields evidence for Acheuleanoccupation. Rock art engravings (petroglyphs) are present on laterite platforms and granite boulders in Usgalimal near the west flowing Kushavati river and in Kajur. In Kajur, the rock engravings of animals, tectiforms and other designs in granite have been associated with what is considered to be a megalithic stone circle with a round granite stone in the centre.Petroglyphs, cones, stone-axe, and choppers dating to 10,000 years ago have been found in various locations in Goa, including Kazur, Mauxim, and the Mandovi-Zuari basin. Evidence of Palaeolithic life is visible at Dabolim, Adkon, Shigao, Fatorpa, Arli, Maulinguinim, Diwar, Sanguem, Pilerne, and Aquem-Margaon. Difficulty in carbon dating the laterite rock compounds poses a problem for determining the exact time period.

Gold coins issued by the Kadamba king of Goa, Shivachitta Paramadideva. Circa *1147–1187 AD.*

Early Goan society underwent radical change when Indo-Aryan and Dravidian migrants amalgamated with the aboriginal locals, forming the base of early Goan culture.

In the 3rd century BC, Goa was part of the Maurya Empire, ruled by the Buddhist emperor, Ashoka of Magadha. Buddhist monks laid the foundation of Buddhism in Goa. Between the 2nd century BC and the 6th century AD, Goa was ruled by the Bhojas of Goa. Chutus of Karwar also ruled some parts as feudatories of the Satavahanas of Kolhapur (2nd century BC to the 2nd century AD), Western Kshatrapas (around 150 AD), the Abhiras of Western Maharashtra, Bhojas of the Yadav clans of Gujarat, and the Konkan Mauryas as feudatories of the Kalachuris. The rule later passed to the Chalukyas of Badami, who controlled it between 578 and 753, and later the Rashtrakutas of Malkhed from 753 to 963. From 765 to 1015, the Southern Silharas of Konkan ruled Goa as the feudatories of the Chalukyas and the Rashtrakutas. Over the next few centuries, Goa was successively ruled by the Kadambasas the feudatories of the Chalukyas of Kalyani. They patronised Jainism in Goa.

In 1312, Goa came under the governance of the Delhi Sultanate. The kingdom's grip on the region was weak, and by 1370 it was forced to surrender it to Harihara I of the Vijayanagara empire. The Vijayanagara monarchs held on to the territory until 1469, when it was appropriated by the Bahmani sultans of Gulbarga. After that dynasty crumbled, the area fell into the hands of the Adil Shahis of Bijapur, who established as their auxiliary capital the city known under the Portuguese as Velha Goa (or Old Goa).

The Se Cathedral at Old Goa, an example of Portuguese architecture and one of the largest churches in Asia.

The Mahadeva Temple, attributed to the Kadamba period.

In 1510, the Portuguese defeated the ruling Bijapur sultan Yusuf Adil Shah with the help of a local ally, Timayya. They set up a permanent settlement in Velha Goa. This was the beginning of Portuguese rule in Goa that would last for four and a half centuries, until its annexation in 1961. The Goa Inquisition, a formal tribunal, was established in 1560, and was finally abolished in 1812.

In 1843 the Portuguese moved the capital to Panaji from Velha Goa. By the mid-18th century, Portuguese Goa had expanded to most of the present-day state limits. Simultaneously the Portuguese lost other possessions in India until their borders stabilised and formed the Estado da Índia Portuguesa or *State of Portuguese India*, of which Goa was the largest territory.

After India gained independence from the British in 1947, India requested that Portuguese territories on the Indian subcontinent be ceded to India. Portugal refused to negotiate on the sovereignty of its Indian enclaves. On 19 December 1961, the Indian Army invaded with Operation Vijay resulting in the annexation of Goa, and of Daman and Diu islands into the Indian union. Goa, along with Daman and Diu, was organised as a centrally administered union territory of India. On 30 May 1987, the union territory was split, and Goa was made India's twenty-fifth state, with Daman and Diu remaining a union territory.

Earliest history

There is evidence of the tectonic origins of Goa dating back to 10,000 BC. Further, evidence of human occupation of Goa dates back at least to the Lower Paleolithic Age, indicated by the archaeological findings of Acheulean bifaces in the Mandovi-Zuari basin. However, evidence suggesting the region's ancient foundation is obscured by the legend of Goa's creation by the Hindu sage Parashurama.

Geological origins

Some parts of present-day Goa appear to have been uplifted from the sea due to geological tectonic plate movement. There is evidence to support this theory as indicated by presence of marine fossils, buried seashells and other features of reclaimed topography in the coastal belt. The evidence provided by the conch shells at Surla village, fossilized marine conch shells discovered in 1863, petrified roots, fossilized branches have been found later in many villages on the foothills of the Sahyadri dating back more than 10,000 BC. Thus the geologists concluded that Goa has risen up from seabed as a result of violent tectonic movements. At the decline of the intensity of *pluviation* in the last *Pleistocenic age* around 10.000 BC, the bottom of Deccan plateau was lifted up and out of sea-waters by the tectonic movements, formed the West-coast of India, Goa being a part thereof.

Vedic origins

Multiple places mentioned in ancient Sanskrit texts - *Gomanta*, *Govarashtra*, *Govapuri* and *Gomanchal* - have been interpreted as references to Goa. The prefix common to all of these names is *go*, which means cow in Sanskrit. The suffixes translate to country (*rashtra*), city (*puri*) and shelter (*anchal*).

The first literary reference to Goa is in the Bhishma Parva of Mahabharata as *Gomanta* which translates as the region of cows. A legend states Lord Krishna defeated Jarasandha, the king of Magadha on Gomanchal Mountain, identified as a location in Goa.

Suta Samhita section of Skanda Purana mentions Goa as *Govapuri*

Govapuri is mentioned in Sahyadrikhanda of Skanda Purana, which says the extent of *Govapuri* was about seven *Yojanas*.

According to the Parshurama samhita, Parashurama, the sixth reincarnation of Vishnu faced with an order of banishment from the lands that he had once conquered, sets seven arrows fly from the Sahydris to push back the sea and create a stretch of land which he could claim for himself. The sea-god is believed to have acceded his to wish and created a region *Shurparaka*, which translates literally to winnowing fan. This region is also known as *Parashurama Kshetra*. The legend further tells us that having created Goa, Parashurama brought Goud Saraswat Brahmins from the North and settled them in this land.(See:*Shree Scanda Puran (Sayadri Khandha)*-Ed. Dr. Jarson D. Kunha, Marathi version Ed. By Gajananshastri Gaitonde).The Parashurama samhita thus serves as a symbol of the Sanskritisation that Goan culture experienced with the advent of Brahminical religion to the region, and establishment of Brahminical hegemony

PREHISTORIC PERIOD

Paleolithic and Mesolithic era

Until 1993 the existence of humans in Goa during the Paleolithic and Mesolithic period was highly debated. The discovery of rock art engravings on lateritic platforms and granite boulders from *Usgalimal* on the banks of west-flowing river Kushavati River, has shed light on the prehistory of Goa. The rock shelter at Usgalimal has enough space for 25 to 30 people. The perennial stream in the vicinity which might have served Stone age man for centuries as a source of water. An anthropomorphic figure of Mother goddess and tectiforms resembling tree-like motifs have been found. This site was discovered by Dr P.P.Shirodkar. Exploration of several Mesolithic sites of the Mandovi-Zuari basin, at other sites such as Keri, Thane, Anjuna, *Mauxim*, *Kazur* in Quepem, *Virdi*, has led to the discovery of several scrapers, points, bores, cones, et cetera. A hand axe has also been found at Usgalimal. Further *unifacial* choppers were recovered on a flat-based pebble of quartzite from a pebble conglomerate at *Shigaon* on the Dudhsagar River. Shirodakar made a detailed study of the rock engravings and dated them to Upper paleolithic and Mesolithic phases, or to 20,000-30,000 BC. These discoveries have demonstrated that the region had been supporting a population of hunter-gatherers well before the advent of agriculture. Evidence of Palaeolithic cave existence can be seen at Dabolim, Adkon, Shigaon, Fatorpa, Arli, Maulinguinim, Diwar, Sanguem, Pilerne, Aquem-Margaon et cetera. Difficulty in carbon dating the laterite rock compounds has posed a problem in determining the exact time period.

Kushavati Shamanic culture

Dr. Nandkumar Kamat from the University of Goa discovered the prehistoric petroglyphs of Goa. More than 125 forms were found scattered on the banks of river Kushavati in south-eastern Goa. According to Kamat, these are evidence of a prehistoric Goan shamanistic practice. For hundreds of years, the Kushavati rock art of Goa was known locally as *goravarakhnyachi chitram,* or pictures made by cowherds. But people did not know how ancient the works were, nor could anyone interpret them. After thorough study of these forms, scholars have concluded that these petroglyphs differ from those found elsewhere in Goa. Deeper studies and analysis over a period of ten years showed these petroglyphs were an exquisitely carved *ocular labyrinth*, one of the best in India and Asia. Its ocular nature added to the evidence of prehistoric shamanism.

The studies have shown that the Kushavati culture was a hunter-gatherer culture with deep knowledge of local natural resources and processes - water, fish, plants, game, animal breeding cycles, seasons and natural calamities. The Kushavati culture was greatly concerned with water security, so they set up camps near the streams. The Kushavati found food security in the jungle near the steam. Like every culture, its members confronted the mysteries of illness, death and birth. Kamat believes that this culture dated to 6,000 to 8,000 years ago. On basis of recent DNA-based work on human migration, Dr.

Nandkumar Kamat has ruled out the possibility of Kushavati shamans belonging to the first wave of humans to arrive in Goa. They were not negritoes or austrics. Most probably they were the earliest Mediterraneans who had descended the Western Ghats, probably in their search for sea salt on Goa's coast. As the Kushavati transitioned into a Neolithic society, they began the domestication of animals and were in the last phase of using stone tools. The entire realm of shamanism underwent a radical transition. Today evidence of the metamorphosis in masked dance drama *Perni jagor* can be seen in the same cultural region.

Neolithic period

Archaeological evidence in the form of polished stone axes, suggest the first settlements of Neolithic man in Goa. These axes have been found in Goa Velha.During this period tribes of Austric origin such as the *Kols*, *Mundaris* and *Kharvis* may have settled Goa, living on hunting, fishing and a primitive form of agriculture since 3500 BC. According to Goan historian Anant Ramakrishna Dhume, the Gauda and Kunbi and other such castes are modern descendants of ancient Mundari tribes. Dhume notes several words of Mundari origin in the Konkani language. He describes the deities worshipped by the ancient tribes, their customs, methods of farming, and its overall effect on modern-day Goan culture. The Negroids were in a Neolithic stage of primitive culture and were food-gatherers. Traces of Negroid physical characteristics can be found in parts of Goa, up to at least the middle of the first millennium.

The Proto-Australoid tribe known as the *Konkas*, from whom is derived the name of the region, *Kongvan or Konkan,* with the other mentioned tribes, reportedly made up the earliest settlers in the territory. Agriculture had not fully developed at this stage and was being developed. The Kol and Mundari may have been using stone and wood implements, as iron implements were used by the megalithic tribes as late as 1200 BC. The Kol tribe is believed to have migrated from Gujarat.

During this period, the people began worship of a mother goddess in the form of anthill or *Santer*. The Anthill is called *Roen*(Konkani:0K/#), which is derived from the Austric word *Rono,* meaning with holes. The later Indo-Aryan and Dravidian settlers also adopted anthill worship, which was translated into Prakrit *Santara*. They also worshipped the mother earth by the name of *Bhumika* in Prakrit. Anthill worship still continues in Goa.

THE IRON AGE

The Formations of Gaumkaris and the self rule

The theocratic democracy of Sumer was transformed into the oligarchic democracy of village-administration in Goa known as *Gaumkari*, when it overlapped with the practices of the locals. The agricultural land was jointly owned by the group of villagers, they had right to auction the land, this rent was used for development, and the remainder was distributed amongst the *Gaukars.*

Sumerians view that the village land must belong to the village god or goddess, this was the main feature of the *Gaumkari* system where the village's preeminent deity's temple was the centre of all the activities. It consisted of definite boundaries of land from village to village with its topographic detail, its management and social, religious and cultural interaction. Gaumkari thus were in existence long before constitution of the state of Goa itself.

Thus even before any king ruled the territory, oligarchic democracy in the form of Gaumkari existed in Goa. This form of village-administration was called as *Gaumponn*, and despite the periodic change of sovereigns, the Gaumponn always remained, hence the attachment and fidelity of the Goans to their village has always surpassed their loyalty to their rulers (most of them were extraterritorial). This system for governance became further systematised and fortified, and it has continued to exist ever since. Even today 223 comunidades are still functioning in Goa, though not in the true sense.

The later migrations

The second wave of migrants arrived sometime between 1700 and 1400 BC. This second wave migration was accompanied by southern Indians from the Deccan plateau. A wave of *Kusha* or Harappan people moved to Lothal probably around 1600 BC to escape submergence of their civilisation which thrived on sea-trade.With the admixture of several cultures, customs, religions, dialects and beliefs, led to revolutionary change in early Goan society.

THE AGE OF EMPIRES

The Mauryas

The history of the Mauryas is almost non-existent. The existing records disclose the names of only three of the dynasty's kings, namely *Suketavarman*, who ruled some time in the 4th or 5th centuries BC, *Chandravarman* in the 6th century BC, and *Ajitavarman* in the 7th century BC, who ruled from *Kumardvipa* or modern *Kumarjuve*, but beyond that the records provide no clue as to their mutual relationship. These dates were determined by comparing the style of the Nagari script in which these records are written with the evolution of this script, which may be dated fairly accurately. It is possible to infer from the places mentioned in these records and their discovery locations that at its zenith, the Western Maurya Kingdom comprised the Lata or South Gujarat, coastal Maharashtra, Goa, and approximately half of the North Kanara district. After the Maurya Empire had passed its meridian in the 2nd century BC its satrap in Aparanta made himself independent. A scion of the imperial Mauryas, he founded a dynasty that ruled over the west coast for nearly four centuries from its capital *Shurparaka* or modern Sopara. This dynasty was known as the *Konkan Mauryas*. Goa was called *Sunaparant* by the Mauryas.

Chandragupta Maurya incorporated the west coast of India in his province of Aparanta, and the impact of Magadhan Prakrit, the official language of the Mauryan Empire, on the local dialects resulted in the formation of early Konkani, as was the case with other Aryan vernaculars.

During this era Buddhism was introduced to Goa. Similarly a native Goan named Purna, also known as Punna in Pali, who traveled to Sarnath is considered a direct disciple of Buddha, who popularised Buddhism in Goa in 5th century BC.

The Shatavahanas

The Satavahana dynasty began as vassals of the Mauryan Empire, but declared independence as the Mauryan Empire declined.

The Satavahana dynasty ruled Goa through their coastal vassals, the Chutus of Karwar. This period is estimated to have lasted from around the 2nd century BC to 100 AD. The Satavahanas had established maritime power and their contacts with Roman empire from the coastal trade from Sindh to Saurashtra, from Bharuch to Sopara to Goa, where Greek and Roman ships would halt during voyages.

The Bhojas fortified themselves after the end of Satavahana Empire. With the fall of the Satavahanas, the lucrative seaborne trade declined. Many Greek converts to Buddhism settled in Goa during this period. Buddha statues in Greek styles have been found in Goa. It can be seen that they ruled a very small part of Goa. Maharashtri *prakrit* was their language of administration, which influenced medieval Konkani to a great extent.

Goa under the Western Kshatrapas

In the year 150AD, Vashishtiputra Satakarni was defeated by his son-in-law, the Kshatrapa King Rudradaman I who established his rule over Goa. This dynasty ruled the territory until 249AD. Thereafter the dynasty's power seems to have been weakened by their generals, the Abhiras

Bhojas

First existing as vassals of the Mauryan Empire and later as an independent empire, the Bhojas ruled Goa for more than 500 years, annexing the entirety of Goa.

The earliest known record of the Bhoja Empire from Goa dates from the 4th century AD, it was found in the town of Shiroda in Goa. According to Puranik, by tradition the Bhojas belonged to the clan of Yadavas, who may have migrated to Goa via Dwaraka after the Mahabharata war. Two Bhoja copperplates grants dating back to the 3rd century BC were unearthed from Bandora village, written by King Prithvimallavarman. Many other copper plates, have also been recovered from other places in Goa which date from the 3rd century BC to the 8th century AD. Ancient *Chandrapur*, modern day Chandor, was the capital of the Bhoja Empire; the Bhojas ruled Goa, Belgaum and North Canara.

From the Bhoja inscriptions found in Goa and Konkan, it is evidenced that the Bhojas used Sanskrit and Prakrit for administration. According to Vithal Raghavendra Mitragotri, many Brahmins and Vaishyas arrived with Kshatriyas Bhojas from the north. The Kshatriya Bhojas patronised Buddhism and employed many Buddhist converts of Greek and Persian origin.

MEDIEVAL PERIOD

Goa was ruled by several dynasties of various origins from the 1st century BC to 1500 AD. Since Goa had been under the sway of several dynasties, there was no organised judicial or policing system in those days, except for traditional arrangements governed by absolute rulers and local chieftains. There may have been more order under Muslim rule. During this time, Goa was not ruled as a singular kingdom. Parts of this territory were ruled by several different kingdoms. The boundaries of these kingdoms were not clearly defined and the kings were content to consider their dominions as extending over many villages, which paid tribute and owed them allegiance.

Dynasties controlling Goa from the 1st century BC to 1500 AD

Name of the ruler	Reign
Indo-Parthians	2nd–4th centuries AD
Abhiras, Batapuras, Bhojas	4th–6th centuries
Chalukyas of Badami	6th–8th centuries
Rashtrakutas of Malkhed, Shilaharas	8th–10th centuries
Kadambas	1006–1356
Yadavas of Devagiri	12th and 13th centuries
Vijayanagar Empire	14th and 15th centuries
Bahmani Sultanate	15th century

Shilaharas

The Shilaharas of South Konkan ruled Goa from 755 until 1000 AD. Sannaphulla, the founder of the dynasty, was a vassal of the Rashtrakutas. Their copper-plate inscriptions suggest that they ruled from Vallipattana (there is no unanimity amongst the scholars regarding identification of Vallipattana, some identify it with Balli in Goa, or it may either be Banda or Kharepatan in the modern-day state of Maharashtra), Chandrapura and Gopakapattana. This was a tumultuous period in Goan history. As the Goa Shilahara power waned during the 11th century, the Arab traders gained increasing control of the overseas trade. They enjoyed autonomy from the Shilaharas. In order to control this decline, Kadamba King Guhalladeva I, ruling from Chandor, established secular, political, and economic partnerships with these Arab states. After the Chalukyas defeated the Rashtrakutas, exploiting this situation to their advantage, the Kadamba King, Shashthadeva II, firmly established his rule in Goa.

Kadambas

The Kadambas ruled Goa between the 10th and 14th centuries. In the beginning, the Kadambas ruled only Sashti present day Salcette, a small part of Konkan. They ruled from

Chandor, over a large part of Goa, but the port of Gopakapattana was not included in the early years.

Port of Goapakapattna

Later King Shashthadeva conquered the island of Goa, including the ports of Gopakpattana and Kapardikadvipa, and annexed a large part of South Konkan to his kingdom. He made Gopakpattana as his secondary capital. His successor, King Jayakeshi I, expanded the Goan kingdom. The Sanskrit Jain text *Dvayashraya*mentions the extent of his capital. Port Gopakapattna had trade contacts with Zanzibar, Bengal, Gujarat and Sri Lanka (mentioned as Zaguva, Gauda, Gurjara, and Simhala in the Sanskrit texts). The city has been described in the contemporary records not only as aesthetically pleasing, but spiritually cleansing as well. Because it was a trading city, Gopakapattna was influenced by many cultures, and its architecture and decorative works showed this cosmopolitan effect. The capital was served by an important highway called Rajvithi or Rajpath, which linked it with Ela, the ruins of which can still be seen. For more than 300 years, it remained a centre for intra-coastal and trans-oceanic trade from Africa to Malaya. Later in the 14th century, the port was looted by the Khalji general Malik Kafur. The capital was transferred to Chandor and then back to Gopakapattna because of Muhammad bin Tughluq's attack on Chandor.

Guhalladeva III, Jayakeshi II, Shivachitta Paramadideva, Vinshuchitta II and Jayakeshi III dominated Goa's political scene in the 12th century. During the rule of Kadambas, the name and fame of Goapuri had reached it zenith. Goa's religion, culture, trade and arts flourished under the rule of these kings. The Kings and their queens built many Shiva temples as they were devout Shaivites. They assumed titles like Konkanadhipati, Saptakotisha Ladbha Varaveera, Gopakapura varadhishva, Konkanmahacharavarti and Panchamahashabda. The Kings had matrimonial relationships with the Kings of Saurashtra, and even the local chieftains. The Kings patronised Vedic religion and performed major fire sacrifices like *the horse sacrifice* or

Ashvamedha. They are also known for patronising Jainism in Goa.

Though their language of administration was Sanskrit and Kannada, Konkani and Marathi were also prevalent. They introduced Kannada language to Goa, which had a very profound influence on the local tongue. Nagari script, Kadamba script, Halekannada script and Goykanadi scripts were very popular. Kadamba Tribhuvanamalla, inscribed a record, dated saka 1028 or AD 1106, that he established a Brahmapuri at Gopaka. Brahmapuris were ancient universities run by the Brahmins where the Vedas, astrology, philosophy, medicine, and other subjects were studied. Such Brahampuris were found in many places in Goa such as Savoi verem and Gauli moula.

Kadambas ruled Goa for more than 400 years. On 16 October 1345 Goa Kadamba King Suriya Deva was assassinated by Muslim invaders.

Bahmani Sultanate

In 1350 AD, Goa was ruled by the Bahmani Sultanate. However, in 1370, the Vijayanagar empire, a resurgent Hindu empire situated at modern day Hampi, reconquered the area. The Vijayanagar rulers held on to Goa for nearly a century, during which time its harbours were important port of arrival for Arabian horses on their way to Hampi to strengthen the Vijaynagar cavalry. In 1469 Goa was reconquered by the Bahmani Sultans of Gulbarga. When this Sultanate broke up in 1492, Goa became a part of Adil Shah's Bijapur Sultanate, which established Goa Velha as its second capital. The former Secretariat building in Panaji is a former Adil Shahi palace, later taken over by the Portuguese Viceroys as their official residence.

Portuguese rule and Colonial Invasion Of Goa

Vasco da Gama joined the Portuguese navy as a young man, where he learned navigational skills and served with distinction in the war against Castile. He set off from Lisbon in 1497 and a year later, landed in Calicut, India, and broke the Arab monopoly of trade.

A breech-loading swivel gunthought to have been constructed in the 16th century in Portuguese Goa, India. Caliber: 95mm, length: 2880mm. It was exported to Japan and used in the time of Oda Nobunaga.

In 1510, Portuguese admiral Afonso de Albuquerque attacked Goa at the behest of the local chieftain Timayya. After losing the city briefly to its former ruler, Ismail Adil Shah, the Muslim King of Bijapur, Albuquerque returned in force on 25 November, with a fully renovated fleet. In less than a day, the Portuguese fleet took possession of Goa from Ismail Adil Shah and his Ottoman allies, who surrendered on 10 December. It is estimated that 6,000 of the 9,000 Muslim defenders of the city died, either in the battle in the streets or while trying to escape. Albuquerque gained the support of the Hindu population, although this frustrated the initial expectations of Thimayya, who aspired to control the city. Afonso de Albuquerque rewarded him by appointing him chief *Aguazil* of the city, an administrator and representative of the Hindu and Muslim people; he was a learned interpreter of the local customs. Albuquerque made an agreement to lower yearly dues and taxes. In spite of frequent attacks by raiders, Goa became the centre of Portuguese India, with the conquest triggering the compliance of neighboring kingdoms; the Sultan of Gujarat and the Zamorin of Calicut dispatched embassies, offering alliances and local concessions to be fortified.

In Goa, Albuquerque started the first Portuguese mint in the East, after complaints from merchants and Timoja about the scarcity of currency. He used it as an opportunity to announce the territorial conquest by the design of the new coins. The new coin, based on the existing local coins, bore a cross on one side and the design of an armillary sphere (or *esfera*), King Manuel's badge, on the reverse. Gold, silver and bronze coins were issued: gold *cruzados* or *manueis*, *esperas* and *alf-esperas*, and *leais*. More mints were built in Malacca in 1511.

Albuquerque and his successors left the customs and constitutions of the thirty village communities on the island almost untouched, abolishing only the rite of *sati*, in which widows were burned on their husband's funeral pyre. A register of these customs (*Foral de usos e costumes*) was published in 1526; it is among the most valuable historical documents pertaining to Goan customs.

Goa was the base for Albuquerque's conquest of Malacca in 1511 and Hormuz in 1515. Albuquerque intended it to be a colony and a naval base, distinct from the fortified factories established in certain Indian seaports. Goa was made capital of the Portuguese Vice-Kingdom in Asia, and the other Portuguese possessions in India, Malacca and other bases in Indonesia, East Timor, the Persian Gulf, Macau in China and trade bases in Japan were under the suzerainty of its Viceroy. By mid–16th century, the area under occupation had expanded to most of present-day limits.

Goa was granted the same civic privileges as Lisbon. Its senate or municipal chamber maintained direct communications with the king and paid a special representative to attend to its interests at court. In 1563 the governor proposed to make Goa the seat of a parliament representing all parts of the Portuguese east, but this was rejected by the King.

The Portuguese set up a base in Goa to consolidate their control of the lucrative spice trade. Goods from all parts of the East were displayed in its bazaar, and separate streets were designated for the sale of different classes of goods: Bahrain pearls and coral, Chinese porcelain and silk, Portuguese velvet and piece-goods, and drugs and spices from the Malay Archipelago.

In 1542, St. Francis Xavier mentions the architectural

splendour of the city. It reached the height of its prosperity between 1575 and 1625. Travellers marvelled at *Goa Dourada*, or Golden Goa. A Portuguese proverb said, "He who has seen Goa need not see Lisbon."

In the main street, African and Indian slaves were sold by auction. The houses of the rich were surrounded by gardens and palm groves; they were built of stone and painted red or white. Instead of glass, their balconied windows had thin polished oyster-shells set in lattice-work. The social life of Goa's rulers befitted the capitol of the viceregal court, the army and navy, and the church; luxury and ostentation became a byword before the end of the 16th century.

Almost all manual labour was performed by slaves. The common soldiers assumed high-sounding titles, and even the poor noblemen who congregated in boarding-houses subscribed for a few silken cloaks, a silken umbrella and a common man-servant, so that each could take his turn to promenade the streets, fashionably attired and with a proper escort.

Around 1583, missionary activity in Cuncolim led to conflicts, culminating in the Cuncolim Revolt in which natives killed all the missionaries. The Portuguese authorities called the sixteen chieftains of each ward or *vado* of the Cuncolim village to the Assolna Fort, ostensibly to form a peace pact with the villagers. At the fort the Portuguese killed the chieftains, except for two who jumped from the fort into the Arabian Sea and presumably swam to Karwar. The villagers lost their traditional leaders and the Portuguese began confiscating the land of the locals. At the same time, they initiated the Goa Inquisition.

In 1556 the printing press was first introduced to India and Asia at Saint Paul's College in Goa; through the spread of the printing press, Goa led the acceleration of the availability of the knowledge and customs of Europe. After getting established in Goa, the Jesuits introduced the printing press technology for the first time in history into Macau-China in 1588 and into Japan in 1590. The Jesuits founded the university of Santo Tomas in the Philippines, which is the oldest existing university in Asia; in the same period, Goa Medical College was established as the first European medical college in Asia.

The Crown in Lisbon undertook to finance missionary activity; missionaries and priests converted large numbers of people in all spheres of society, especially in Goa. St Francis Xavier in Goa, pioneered the establishment of a seminary, called Saint Paul's College. It was the first Jesuit headquarters in Asia. St Francis founded the College to train Jesuit missionaries. He went to the Far East, traveling towards China. Missionaries of the Jesuit Order spread out through India, going as far north as the court of the great Moghul Emperor Jallaluddin Akbar. Having heard about the Jesuits, he invited them to come and teach him and his children about Christianity.

From Goa, the Jesuit order was able to set up base almost anywhere in Asia for evangelistic missions, including the founding of Roman Catholic colleges, universities and faculties of education. Jesuits are known for their work in education, intellectual research, and cultural pursuits, and for their missionary efforts. Jesuits also give retreats, minister in hospitals and parishes, and promote social justice and ecumenical dialogue.; Saint Paul's College Goa was a base for their evangelisation of Macau, and then for their important missionary campaigns into China and Japan. Macau eventually superseded St Paul's College, Goa. They built St Paul College in 1594 (now the University of Macau), known in Latin as the college of *Mater Dei*. Because of state conflicts with the Jesuits, In 1762 the Marquês de Pombal expelled the order from Macau. The Macau university combined evangelisation with education.

In the year 1600 António de Andrade made the long voyage from Lisbon to Goa, where he pursued his higher studies at St. Paul's College and was ordained a Jesuit priest. He eventually became rector of the same college. He made a landmark missionary expedition from Goa, across the length of India and into Tibet. He overcame incredible hardships in the journey as the first European to cross the Himalaya mountains into Tibet. There he founded churches and a mission in 1625. The corpse of the co-founder of the Society of Jesus, Francis Xavier, whose example many Goan missionaries tried to emulate by engaging in evangelising work in Asia, was shipped to Goa on 11 December 1553. Goa has also produced its own saints: the martyrs of Cuncolim; St. Joseph Vaz, whose missionary exploits in Sri Lanka are remembered with gratitude in that country; and the Venerable Angelo de Souza.

The 16th-century monument, the Cathedral or Sé, was constructed during Portugal's Golden Age, and is the largest church in Asia, as well as larger than any church in Portugal. The church is 250 ft in length and 181 ft in breadth. The frontispiece stands 115 ft high. The Cathedral is dedicated to St. Catherine of Alexandria and is also known as St. Catherine's Cathedral. It was on her feast day in 1510 that Afonso de Albuquerque defeated the Muslim army and took possession of the city of Goa.

The Goa Inquisition was the office of the Inquisition acting within the Indian state of Goa and the rest of the Portuguese empire in Asia. It was established in 1560, briefly suppressed from 1774–1778, and finally abolished in 1812. The Goan Inquisition is considered a blot on the history of Roman Catholic Christianity in India by both Christians and non-Christians alike. Based on the records that survive, H. P. Salomon and I. S. D. Sassoon state that between the Inquisition's beginning in 1561 and its temporary abolition in 1774, some 16,202 persons were brought to trial. Of this number, only 57 were sentenced to death and executed; another 64 were burned in effigy. Most were subjected to lesser punishments or penances.

The Inquisition was established to punish relapsed New Christians, Jews and Muslims who had converted to Catholicism, as well as their descendants, but were suspected of practicing their ancestral religion in secret. Numerous Portuguese Jews (as converted Catholics) had come to Goa and worked as traders. Due to persecution during the Inquisition, most left and migrated to Fort St. George (later Madras/Chennai) and Cochin, where English and Dutch rule, respectively, were more tolerant.

In Goa the Inquisition also scrutinised Indian converts from Hinduism or Islam who were thought to have returned to their original ways. It prosecuted non-converts who broke prohibitions against the observance of Hindu or Muslim rites, or interfered with Portuguese attempts to convert non-Christians to Catholicism. While its ostensible goal was to preserve the Catholic faith, the Inquisition was used against Indian Catholics as an instrument of social control, as well as a method of confiscating victims' property and enriching the Inquisitors. Goan Inquisition was abolished in 1812.

Decline

The appearance of the Dutch in Indian waters was followed by the gradual ruin of Goa. In 1603 and 1639, the city was blockaded by Dutch fleets, though never captured. In 1635 Goa was ravaged by an epidemic.

Trade was gradually monopolised by the Jesuits. Jean de Thévenot in 1666, Baldaeus in 1672, and Fryer in 1675 describe Goa's ever-increasing poverty and decay. After escaping from Agra, Shivaji slowly started gaining the areas which he lost through the Treaty of Purendar to the Moghuls. He conquered most of the area adjoining the Old Conquestas of Goa. He captured Pernem, Bicholim, Sattari, Ponda, Sanguem, Quepem and Canacona. Sawantwadi Bhonsale and Saudekar Rajas became his vassals.

In 1683 Sambhaji, the son of Shivaji, tried to conquer all of Goa, including the areas then in Portuguese control. He almost ousted the Portuguese, but to their surprise a Mughal army prevented the city's capture by the Marathas. In 1739 the whole territory of Bardez was attacked by the Marathas again in order to pressure the northern Portuguese possession at Vasai, but the conquest could not be completed because of the unexpected arrival of a new viceroy with a fleet.

In June 1756 Luís Mascarenhas, Count of Alva(Conde de Alva), the Portuguese Viceroy was killed in action by Maratha Army in Goa. Following the Third Battle of Panipat, Peshawa control over Maratha Empire was weakened. The Portuguese defeated the Rajas of Sawantwadi and the Raja of Sunda to conquer an area that stretched from Pernem to Cancona. This territory formed the Novas Conquistas, the boundaries of present-day Goa.

In the same year the viceroy transferred his residence from the vicinity of Goa city to New Goa (in Portuguese *Nova Goa*), today's Panaji. In 1843 this was made the official seat of government in 1843; it completed a move that had been discussed as early as 1684. Old Goa city's population fell steeply during the 18th century as Europeans moved to the new city. Old Goa has been designated a World Heritage Site by UNESCO because of its history and architecture.

In 1757, King Joseph I of Portugal issued a decree, developed by his minister Marquês de Pombal, granting Portuguese citizenship and representation to all subjects in the Portuguese Indies. The enclaves of Goa, Damão, Diu, Dadra and Nagar Haveli became collectively known as the *Estado da Índia Portuguesa*, and were represented in the Portuguese parliament. (The first election was held in Goa on 14 Jan 1822, electing 3 locals as members of Parliament.)

In 1787, some priests started a rebellion against Portuguese rule. It was known as the Conspiracy of the Pintos. Goa was peacefully occupied by the British between 1812-1815 in line with the Anglo-Portuguese Alliance during the Napoleonic Wars.

Second World War

Goa remained neutral during the conflict like Portugal. As a result, at the outbreak of hostilities a number of Axis ships sought refuge in Goa rather than be sunk or captured by the British Royal Navy. Three German merchants ships, the *Ehrenfels*, the *Drachenfels* and the *Braunfels*, as well as an Italian ship, took refuge in the port of Mormugao. The *Ehrenfels* began transmitting Allied ship movements to the U-boats operating in the Indian Ocean, an action that was extremely damaging to Allied shipping.

But the British Navy was unable to take any official action against these ships because of Goa's stated neutrality. Instead the Indian mission of SOE backed a covert raid using members from the Calcutta Light Horse, a part-time unit made up of civilians who were not eligible for normal war service. The Light Horse embarked on an ancient Calcutta riverboat, the *Phoebe*, and sailed round India to Goa, where they sunk the *Ehrenfels*. The British then sent a decrypted radio message announcing it was going to seize the territory. This bluff made the other Axis crews scuttle their ships fearing they could be seized by British forces.

The raid was covered in the book *Boarding Party* by James Leasor. Due to the potential political ramifications of the fact that Britain had violated Portuguese neutrality, the raid remained secret until the book was published in 1978. In 1980 the story was made into the film, *The Sea Wolves*, starring Gregory Peck, David Niven and Roger Moore.

AFTER THE INDEPENDENCE OF INDIA

When India became independent in 1947, Goa remained under Portuguese control. The Indian government of Jawaharlal Nehru insisted that Goa, along with a few other minor Portuguese holdings, be turned over to India. However, Portugal refused. By contrast, France, which also had small enclaves in India (most notably Puducherry), surrendered all its Indian possessionsrelatively quickly.

In 1954, unarmed Indians took over the tiny land-locked enclaves of Dadra and Nagar Haveli. This incident led the Portuguese to lodge a complaint against India in the International Court of Justice at The Hague. The final judgement on this case, given in 1960, held that the Portuguese had a right to the enclaves, but that India equally had a right to deny Portugal access to the enclaves over Indian territory.

In 1955 a group of unarmed civilians, the Satyagrahis, demonstrated against Portugal. At least twenty-two of them were killed by Portuguese gunfire.

Later the same year, the Satyagrahis took over a fort at Tiracol and hoisted the Indian flag. They were driven away by the Portuguese with a number of casualties. On 1 September 1955, the Indian consulate in Goa was closed; Nehru declared that his government would not tolerate the Portuguese presence in Goa. India then instituted a blockade against Goa, Damão, and Diu in an effort to force a Portuguese departure. Goa was then given its own airline by the Portuguese, the Transportes Aéreos da Índia Portuguesa, to overcome the blockade.

Indian annexation of Goa

India made many requisitions to the Salazar regime of Portugal to grant their Indian colonies independence, but when that failed, on 18 December 1961, Indian troops crossed the border into Goa and "liberated" it. Operation Vijay involved sustained land, sea and air strikes for more than thirty-six hours; it resulted in the unconditional surrender of Portuguese forces on 19 December. A United Nations resolution "condemning" the invasion was proposed by the United States and the United Kingdom in the United Nations Security Council, but would be vetoed by the USSR. The territory of Goa was under military rule for five months. However, the previous civil service was soon restored. Goan voters went to the polls in a referendum and voted to become an autonomous, federally administered territory. Goa was later admitted Indian statehood in 1987. Goa celebrates "Liberation Day" on 19 December every year, which is also a state holiday.

MEDIA IN GOA

Media in Goa refers to the newspapers, magazines, radio stations, cable and television networks and online media in India's smallest state (3700 square kilometres, population 1.4 million).

Background

Over the years, the media has changed dramatically from its early 20th century beginnings as a battlefield for influential lobbies within the local Catholic society (including caste-based elites, or politically divided groups) which were largely controlled by influential and educated local elites. After the end of Portuguese rule in 1961, new newspapers were set up, which were aligned to the influential local mining lobby. This too has changed in recent years, with some sections of the media becoming more politically aligned, or linked to major business houses both within Goa and its neighbourhood (particularly Maharastra).

Languages

The most widely read newspapers in Goa tend to be published in the English and Marathi languages, with the widely spoken local language of Konkani not receiving much coverage. Konkani-versus-Marathi linguistic battles have led to rivalry between these two language camps around the 1980s. There is friction between the users of the official Devanagari script and the Roman, or Romi script users of Konkani.

Newspapers and magazines

English-language newspapers in Goa comprise: *O Heraldo* (*The Herald*), Goa's oldest newspaper, formerly a Portuguese language daily owned by Raoul Fernandes (Herald Publications Pvt Ltd), a local printing enterprise that grew out of a stationery shop; *The Navhind Times*, published by the mining house of the Dempos since 1963; and the *Gomantak Times*, which changed hands from its earlier owners from the mining house of the Chowgules to the politically-linked Pawar family, based in the neighboring state of Maharashtra. In addition to these, *The Times of India* and *The Indian Express* are also distributed to urban areas from nearby Bombay and Bangalore. A Goan edition of *The Times of India* started publication in June 2008.

The lone English monthly is *Goa Today*, edited by Vinayak Naik and owned by Goa Publications, a firm controlled by the Salgaocars mining house. Other English-language publications include *The Goan*, *Goa Messenger* and the *Goan Observer*.

The First travel magazine of Goa started in Goa in year 2007*Goa Prism*.

Publications in Konkani include *Vauraddeancho Ixtt* (*Workers' Friend*), a weekly magazine in Roman script. In the 1980s, a Roman script Konkani paper called *Novem Goem* folded in large part due to financial difficulties and alleged mismanagement in spite of being set up with enthusiasm and even a drive to collect funds for it through a 'padyatra' (foot-march) across Goa. *Sunaparant* was a Devanagari Konkani daily published which functioned from 1987 to 2015. *The Goan*, which is linked to the industrial house of the Timblos, which has interests in mining and the luxury tourism sector, was started in 2013, edited by Sujay Gupta.

On 15 July 2016, a new Devanagari Konkani daily called "Bhaangar Bhuin" (->0-B/) was established, under the editorship of Pundalik Naik. The daily is published by Fomento Publications.

In the Marathi language, some of the popular newspapers are: the *Tarun Bharat*, which was earlier published from the neighbouring city of Belgaum but now has its presses in Porvorim; the *Daily Pudhari*, which was earlier published from Karaswada, Mapusa; the *Gomantak*, a sister publication of the *Gomantak Times* and much more influential in the past; and *Navprabha* of *The Navhind Times*/Dempo group. Other publications primarily publish "Goa editions" through presses and offices run from outside Goa. Recent years saw the launch of the *Gova Doot*. A nearly three-decade old newspaper, the Marathi daily *Rashtramath* from the South Goa city of Margao suspended publications at the early part of this decade. A new Hindi daily paper *Nitya Samay* also started from Margao. As of 2013, the *Lokmat*, which is a newspaper based in Maharashtra, was also a growing and influential paper in the Marathi segment of the Goa newspaper market; it comes out with a local edition, edited by Raju Nayak.

Out-station dailies reaching Goa from other centres of publication include, *Kesari*, *Maharashtra Times*, *Loksatta*, *The*

Asian Age, *Deccan Herald*, *The Hindu*, *Hindustan Times*, *Navshakti* and more. The two mainstream news agencies operating in the state are the Press Trust of India and the United News of India.

Other publications in the state include *Vasco Watch* (English-language, fortnightly—Free to reader neighbourhood newspaper), *Hello Publications*, *Hello Travel Talk* (English-language, a tourism magazine), *Whats On Goa* (English-language, fortnightly—an event lister Of Goa), *Hello City - Hello Panjim*, *Hello Margao*(English-language), *Hello Goa Yellowpages* (English-language, Yearly), *Gulab* (Konkani, monthly), *Bimb* (Devanagiri-script Konkani), *Poddbimb* (Konkani Roman-script monthly), *Harbour Times*, *[Digital Goa]*, and *J's House* among others. Some of the smaller publications are known to change their name, form or even go out of publication temporarily or permanently.

Radio

Goa was once home to the Emisora Goa, a radio station that was popular when the region was a Portuguese colony. After the end of Portuguese rule, this station was replaced by a station from the All India Radio network. Its studios are at Altinho, the hill-top state-capital Panjim – also known as Panaji, Pangim or Ponnje – and its transmitters are located at Bambolim, some 5 km away. Bambolim also houses transmitters that broadcast foreign-language programmes as part of India's international programme. Two AM channels are broadcast, the primary channel at 1287 kHz and the Vividh Bharati channel at 1539 kHz.

Besides the AM broadcasts, All India Radio has an FM, or frequency modulated, channel called Rainbow FM, broadcasting at 105.4 MHz. Since 2006, the FM channel broadcasts locally produced programs between 4:30 am and 12 midnight. These locally produced programs include mainly English, Konkani and Hindi music. At other times, the channel relays programs from AIR FM Rainbow India channel, providing variety for listeners. It also covers important speeches and events live. Broadcast starts at 6 am and ends at 12:30 am.

Goa has two private FM channels: Big FM and Radio Indigo. Big FM plays only Hindi musics. The channels' programs are hosted in both English and Konkani. The channels have featured Goan artists, like tiatrist Prince Jacob and musician-singer Remo Fernandes. Radio Indigo programming is contemporary international music and international hit music. The music and hosting is in English. Both radio stations broadcast 24 hours a day..

Though the private FM stations have bought life to the radio industry in Goa, signal strength and coverage remain weak in the southern part of Goa, beyond the Verna plateau. Thus, most of the people in south Goa are unable to get reception in their home.

There is also an educational channel, Gyan Vani, run by IGNOU broadcast from Panaji at 105.6 MHz.

Broadcasting background

In the mid-nineties, when India first experimented with private FM broadcasts, the small tourist destination of Goa was the fifth place in the country where private broadcasters could secure FM slots. The first four centres were the major metro cities: Delhi, Mumbai, Kolkata and Chennai.

In Phase-II of FM licensing, Goa's capital, Panjim was categorised as a 'D'-class city, i.e. having a population between 100,000 and 300,000. In the end of January 2006, three private FM radio players won bids to set up private FM radio stations in Goa.:

- Radio Mirchi (ENIL - Times group, linked to the Indian media giant Times of India, Rs 17.1 million;
- Indigo (Jupiter Capital – Rajiv Chandrasekhar, linked to the BPL electronics hardware firm), Rs 12.9 million; and
- Big FM (Adlabs - Reliance – Anil Ambani group) Rs 12.1 million.

Big FM at 92.7 MHz and Radio Mirchi at 98.3 MHz both launched in Goa in May 2007. Radio Indigo at 91.9 MHz, the country's first and only 24hr international hit music station launched in June 2007.

Indian policy stipulates that these bids are a One-Time Entry Fee (OTEF), for the license period of 10 years.

India's earlier attempts to privatise its FM channels ran into difficulty, when most private players bid heavily then could not meet their commitments to pay the governments the expected amounts.

In FM Phase-1 (year 2000), the highest bid in Goa was Rs 41.5 million. Under the policy then, this would have escalated – at 15% each year – to Rs. 146 million by the tenth year of operation. The bidder would have ended up paying Rs. 42.6 crores over 10 years, causing the major players to back off. This time, the only local company from Goa to bid for a license was Tarun Bharat Multigraphics, resulting in all of the winning players being based outside of Goa.

All the three winning bidders were to co-site their transmitting infrastructure with All India Radio's tower on the outskirts of Panaji.

AIR's FM Rainbow has a six kW transmitter, and even this is not heard properly in some distant areas of Goa. The private FM operators are allowed only 3 kW transmitters.

Radio Mirchi (of what was the Times FM group, run by one of the biggest newspaper chains in the country) returned to Goa after many years. In the late 1980s and early 90s, Times FM used to buy air-time on AIR's Panaji FM channel. Radio Mirchi Goa 98.3 was discontinued on 22 May 2017 after its license expired and the company decided not to renew the license due to lack of revenue.

C and D category cities are allowed to network and share programming, but generally, channels prefer to do in-house programming.

News is not permitted on private FM. Nationally, many of the current FM players – like the Times of India, Hindustan

Times, Mid-Day, BBC etc. – are essentially newspaper chains or media, and they are making a strong pitch for News on FM.

St Xavier's College in Mapusa announced the starting of its campus community radio, named Voice of Xavier's (VOX) on 17 December 2006 at 90.4 MHz. The station had a power output of 20 watts. This was Goa's second FM station. It did not however stay in operation apart from test broadcasts. This does not currently operate (as of July 2013).

Television

Goa is served by almost all the television channels available in India. Channels are received through cable in most parts of Goa. In the interior regions, channels are received via satellite dishes.

Doordarshan (DD), the national television broadcaster, has two free terrestrial channels on air: DD National and DD News. DD National broadcasts programmes of short duration in local languages (Konkani, Marathi). Goa has all the cable TV channels generally found in India, namely: MTV, ESPN, Fox, Zee TV, ZEE Marathi, HBO, Star Plus, Star Movies, BBC, CNN, Tensports, AXN, Star World, Star News, Fashion TV, Sony, Set Max, SAB, Sahara One, Sahara News, Discovery Channel, National Geographic Channel, Animal Planet, Channel X5 etc. Electronic media with DTH (Direct To Home) TV services are available from Dish TV, Tata Sky & DD Direct Plus.

Beside these Goa has many major local channels, which cover local events, including political developments, and which reach viewers through the local cable network. These include GOA365 (English /Konkani), Prudent (Konkani), CCR TV (A catholic Religious Channel in English/Konkani) RDXGOA TV(Konkani\English), In Goa News (Marathi\English), Goa Newsline (Konkani), Goa Plus and HCN (English), DBTV a children's educational channel among others. In Goa 24x7 is the only 24-hour live Marathi channel. In April 2015 - Prime Media Goa, a Cable Television Channel has caught the imagination of a large section of the population, not just in Goa but across the globe. The earlier BJP government, at the start of the first decade of this century, officially acknowledged that it was subsidising the operations of some networks, arguing that this was needed to promote programming in the local language

Internet television

In August 2011, a live internet news webcast was commenced by In Goa News.

Most of the Konkani TV channel are available live streaming on the internet. www.konkanitv.ga is one such sites that allows you to watch most of the above television channels live . The other Religious channel, CCR TV is viewable at www.ccr-tv.com

Critiques of the media

Writing in the early 1980s, anthropologist Dr Robert S Newman spoke about the relationship with the media in Goa with the "big families" – mainly comprising "a handful of small-businessmen, traditional landowners, and war profiteers (who) received iron ore mining licenses, and were encouraged to dig and ship the ore to Japan (which needed it for reconstruction after World War II)."

In an essay titled Goa - The Transformation of an Indian Region, published in Pacific Affairs (August 1984) Newman wrote: "[Goa's first post-colonial chief minister Dayanand] Bandodkar and his fellow industrialists attempted to shape public opinion through their newspapers – there are almost no independent papers in Goa – and through tertiary educational institutions which they themselves had established. The Chowgules, for example, launched the newspapers Gomantak and Uzvadd, and were founders of an arts and science college at Margao; the Salgaocars founded a law college; and the Dempos own The Navhind Times and Navprabha, and are involved in Dhempe College at Miramar."

Another essay titled *Popular Protest and the Free Goa Press* (pp 91–113) in Norman Dantas' The Transformation of

Goa (The Other India Press, Mapusa, 1999) argues: "In Goa, the daily newspapers' editorial stances on various protest movements would tend to reveal a largely unfriendly attitude towards such actions.

It is not perhaps coincidental that individuals and groups involved in protest issues in Goa have often felt that they have received an unfair deal from the media." It looks at protest and the media response to it in Goa over a three decade period, from the early 1960s to the 1990s.

2

Culture and Society

CULTURE OF GOA

Goa, a former Portuguese colony, is called 'Rome of the East'. It is considered as the most westernized state of Indian Territory as the inhabitants of Goa adopted western culture. Goa is enriched with cultural heritage that include folk songs, dances, music, visual arts and folk tales. The Goans are fond of football. Environmental issues are prominently featured in Goa.

It is known as a multi-ethnic state with a majority of Hindu and Muslim along with Catholic minority. They live in perfect harmony and participate in each others' religious festivals. Goa is famous for its Indo-Latin festivals especially the carnivals, witnessed by numerous people every year. Other popular festivals observed in Goa are Shigmo- the spring festival and Shivaratri. New Year is celebrated in Goa with great pomp and show.

Nightlife in Goa is alluring. Bars and restaurants are in abundance in Goa as it is the most admired tourist destination of India.

It is also regarded as the dream destination of many foreign tourists. Night-outs and rave parties are held on beaches and nightclubs. Liquor and seafood of Goa attracts the tourists.

Culture of Goa

This chapter is about the culture of natives of the Indian state of Goa. Goans are commonly said to be born with music and football in their blood. This is because football and music are deeply entrenched in Goan culture.

Shanta Durga temple at Kavlem.

Having been a Portuguese territory for over 450 years, Goa's culture is an interesting amalgamation of both Eastern and Western styles, with the latter having a more dominant role. The tableau of Goa showcases religious harmony by focusing on the Deepastambha, the Cross and Ghode Modni followed by a chariot. Western royal attire of kings is as much part of Goa's cultural heritage as are regional dances performed depicting a unique blend of different religions and cultures of this State. Prominent local festivals are Christmas, Easter, Carnival, Diwali, Shigmo, Chavoth, Samvatsar Padvo, Dasara etc. The Goan Carnival and Christmas-new year celebrations are well known to attract a large number of tourists.

The Gomant Vibhushan Award, the highest civilian honour of the State of Goa, is given annually by Government of Goa since 2010.

Dance and music

Traditional Goan art forms are Dekhnni, Fugdi, Corridinho, Mando, Dulpod and Fado. Goan Catholics are fond of social gatherings and Tiatr (Teatro). As part of its Portuguese history, music is an integral part of Goan homes. It is often said that "Goans are born with music and sport". Western musical instruments like the piano, guitars and violins are widely used in most religious and social functions of the Catholics.

Goan Hindus are very fond of Natak, Bhajan and Kirtan. Many famous Indian classical singers hail from Goa, including Mogubai Kurdikar, Kishori Amonkar, Kesarbai Kerkar, Jitendra Abhisheki and Pandit Prabhakar Karekar.

Goa is also known as the origin of Goa trance.

Theatre

Natak, Tiatr (most popular) and Jagor are the chief forms of Goa's traditional performance arts. Other forms are Ranmale, Dashavatari, Kalo, Goulankala, Lalit, Kala and Rathkala. Stories from the Ramayana and the Mahabharata along with more modern social subjects are narrated with song and dance.

"Jagor", the traditional folk dance-drama, is performed by the Hindu Kunbi and Christian Gauda community of Goa, to seek the Devine Grace for protection and prosperity of the crop.

Literal meaning of Jagor is "jagran" or wakeful nights. The strong belief is that the night long performance, awakens the deities once a year and they continue to remain awake throughout the year guarding the village.

Perni Jagor is the ancient mask dance – drama of Goa, performed by Perni families, using well crafted and painted wooden masks, depicting various animals, birds, super natural power, deities, demons and social characters.

Gauda Jagor, is an impression of social life, that displays all the existing moods and modes of human characters. It is predominantly based on three main characters, Gharasher, Nikhandar and Parpati wearing shining dress and headgears. The performance is accompanied by vibrant tunes of Goan folk instruments like Nagara/Dobe, Ghumat, Madale and Kansale.

In some places, Jagor performances are held with participation of both Hindus and Christian community, whereby, characters are played by Hindus and musical support is provided by Christian artistes.

Tiatr (Teatro) and its artists play a major role in keeping the Konkani language & music alive. Tiatr's are conducted solely in the Roman script of Konkani as it is primarily a Christian community based act. They are played in scenes with music at regular intervals, the scenes are portrayals of daily life and are known to depict social and cultural scenarios. Tiatrs are regularly held especially on weekends mainly at Kala Academy, Panaji, Pai Tiatrist Hall at Ravindra Bhavan, Margao and most recent shows have also started at the new Ravindra Bhavan, Baina, Vasco. Western Musical Instruments such as Drums, bass, Keyboards, Trumpets etc. are part of the show and most of them are played acoustically. It is one of Goa's few art forms that is renowned across the world with performances popular among Goans in the Middle-East, Americas and Europe.

Konkani cinema

2005 India Goa Film Festival

Konkani cinema is an Indian film industry, where films are made in the Konkani language, which is spoken mainly in the Indian states of Goa, Maharashtra and Karnataka and to a smaller extent in Kerala. Konkani films have been produced in Goa, Karnataka, Maharashtra and Kerala.

The first full length Konkani film was *Mogacho Anvddo*, released on 24 April 1950, and was produced and directed by A. L.Jerry Braganza, a native of Mapusa, under the banner of ETICA Pictures. Hence, 24 April is celebrated as Konkani Film Day.

Since 2004, starting from the 35th edition, the International Film Festival of India moved its permanent venue to Goa, it is annually held in the months of November and December.

Konkani film Paltadcho manis has been included in the world's best films of 2009 list.

Konkani films are eligible for the National Film Award for Best Feature Film in Konkani. The most commercially successful Konkani film (as of June 2011) is O Maria directed by Rajendra Talak.

In 2012, the whole new change adopted in Konkani Cinema by introducing Digital Theatrical Film "The Victim" directed by Milroy Goes.

Some old Konkani films are *Sukhachem Sopon*, *Amchem Noxib*, *Nirmonn*, *Mhoji Ghorkarn*, *Kortubancho Sonvsar*, *Jivit Amchem Oxem*, *Mog ani Moipas*, *Bhuierantlo Munis*, *Suzanne*, *Boglantt*, *Padri* and *Bhogsonne*. Ujwadu is a 2011 Konkani film directed by Kasargod Chinna and produced by KJ Dhananjaya and Anuradha Padiyar.

Food

Traditional native Goan Fish Curry

Rice with fish curry (*xit koddi* in Konkani) is the staple diet in Goa. Goan cuisine is famous for its rich variety of fish dishes cooked with elaborate recipes. Coconut and coconut oil are widely used in Goan cooking along with chili peppers, spices, and vinegar is used in the Catholic cuisine, giving the food a unique flavour. The Goan cuisine is heavily influenced by Portuguese cuisine.

Goan food may be divided into Goan Catholic and Goan Hindu cuisine with each showing very distinct tastes, characteristics, and cooking styles. Pork dishes such as Vindalho, Xacuti, chouriço, and Sorpotel are cooked for major occasions among the Goan Catholics. An exotic Goan vegetable stew, known as Khatkhate, is a very popular dish during the celebrations of festivals, Hindu and Christian alike. Khatkhate contains at least five vegetables, fresh coconut, and special Goan spices that add to the aroma.

Sannas, *Hitt*, are variants of idli and *Polle*, *Amboli*, and *Kailoleo* are variants of dosa; all are native to Goa. A rich egg-based, multi-layered sweet dish known as bebinca is a favourite at Christmas.

There are some places in Goa which are famous for Goa's traditional & special cuisines. Ros omelette is one of the most popular snacks and street foods in Goa, it is traditionally sold on food carts on streets.

The House of the Seven Gables in Margao

The most popular alcoholic beverage in Goa is feni; cashew feni is made from the fermentation of the fruit of the cashew tree, while coconut feni is made from the sap of toddy palms.

Urrak is another local liquor prepared from Cashew fruit. In fact the bar culture is one of the unique aspects of the Goan villages where a local bar serves as a meeting point for villagers to unwind. Goa also has a rich wine culture.

Architecture

The architecture of Goa is a combination of Goan, Ottoman and Portuguese styles. Since the Portuguese ruled and governed for four centuries, many churches and houses bear a striking element of the Portuguese style of architecture.

Goan Hindu houses do not show any Portuguese influence, though the modern temple architecture is an amalgam of original Goan temple style with Dravidian, Hemadpanthi, Islamic, and Portuguese architecture.

The original Goan temple architecture fell into disuse as the temples were demolished by the Portuguese and the *Sthapati* known as *Thavayi* in Konkani were converted to Christianity though the wooden work and the *Kavi* murals can still be seen.

Religion

Mangueshi Temple, a Hindu temple in Mangueshi, Ponda-Goa.

Goa has a history of communal harmony.

Festivals

The most popular celebrations in the Indian state of Goa are Ganesh Chaturthi (Konkani: *Chavoth*), Diwali, Christmas(Konkani: *Natalam*), Easter (Konkani: *Paskanchem Fest*), Samvatsar Padvo or Sanvsar Padvo, Shigmo, Goa Carnival, (Konkani:*Intruz*) Sao Jao (Feast of John the Baptist) and the biggest feast, Feast of St. Francis Xavier (Goicho Saib). Goa is also known for its New Year's celebrations.Fairs and festivals at various temples are celebrated with great joy. The Goan Carnival is known to attract a large number of tourists.

Education

Cuisine

Rice with fish curry (*Xit kodi* in Konkani) is the staple diet in Goa. Goan cuisine is renowned for its rich variety of fish dishes cooked with elaborate recipes. Coconutand coconut oil is widely used in Goan cooking along with chili peppers, spices and vinegar giving the food a unique flavour. Pork and beef dishes such as Vindaloo, Xacuti and Sorpotel are cooked for major occasions among the Catholics. An exotic Goan vegetable stew, known as Khatkhate, is a very popular dish during the celebrations of festivals, Hindu and Christian alike. Khatkhate contains at least five vegetables, fresh coconut, and special Goan spices that add to the aroma. A rich egg-based multi-layered sweet dish known as bebinca is a favourite at Christmas. The most popular alcoholic beverage in Goa is feni; Cashew feni is made from the fermentation of the fruit of the cashew tree, while coconut feni is made from the sap of toddy palms.

Architecture

Goa has two World Heritage Sites: the Bom Jesus Basilica and a few designated convents. The Basilica holds the mortal remains of St. Francis Xavier, regarded by many Catholics as the patron saint of Goa (the patron of the Archdiocese of Goa is actually St.Joseph Vaz). Once every ten years, the body is taken down for veneration and for public viewing. The last such event was conducted in 2004. The Velhas Conquistas regions are also known for its Goa-Portuguese style architecture.

In many parts of Goa, mansions constructed in the Indo-Portuguese style architecture still stand, though in some villages, most of them are in a dilapidated condition. Fontainhas in Panaji has been declared a cultural quarter, showcasing the life, architecture and culture of Goa. Some influences from the Portuguese era are visible in some of Goa's temples, notably the Mangueshi Temple, although after 1961, many of these were demolished and reconstructed in the indigenous Indian style.

Sports

Football is the most popular sport in Goa, followed by hockey. Cricket, athletics, chess, swimming, table tennis and basketball are other popular sports in Goa. Fishingis also a popular recreational activity.

Arts

Music

Mando and dulpod are traditional goan musical forms.

Goan Hindus are very fond of Natak, Bhajan and Kirtan. Many famous Indian Classical singers hail from Goa, such as, Kishori Amonkar, Kesarbai Kerkar, Jitendra Abhisheki, Prabhakar Karekar.

Many Goans also perform Western classical music

Dance

Some traditional Goan dance forms are dekhnni, fugdi, corridinho and dashavatara. Western social dancing is a part of most celebrations.

Theatre

Goans are very fond of theatre and acting. *Kalo* and *dashavatar* were popular art forms. Marathi Nataks have been very popular among Hindus in Goa for the past two centuries. Tiatr is the major Goan form of theatre common amongst Catholics and is the most commercial offering as it has entertained Goans not only in Goa but also in Mumbai and Pune (which are major cities of India and have a sizeable Goan population) and in the *Gulf* regions of UAE, Kuwait and so on.

Tourism

Goa developed an international reputation in the 1960s as one of the prime stops on the legendary India-Nepal "hippie trail". In the mid-1960s, several Westerners, including "Eight Finger Eddie" walked over the hill to Calangute, and decided to create a community for Westerners. In the early years, Calangute and Baga were the center of this scene, but it grew over the years to include other nearby cities like Anjuna Beach, which became, and arguably still is, the center of the Western youth culture of Goa. By the mid-1980s, there were over 8000 Westerners living in Goa, mostly from Western Europe. The scene was marked by drug culture, trance music and free love. Goa remains today an international center of youth culture.

Starting in the late 1990s, Goa began to attract a more "upscale" audience, which in turn drove prices up, which in turn drove many in the "hippie" community to other less-expensive areas. Arambol—the beach community furthest away from "civilization", like electricity and running water—became the center of a battle between those wanting to turn Goa into a more traditional upscale resort area, and those wanting Goa to retain its traditional rustic counterculture appeal.

MUSIC OF GOA

Music of Goa refers to music from the state of Goa, on the west coast of India. A wide variety of music genres are used in Goa ranging from Western art music to Indian classical music. Konkani music is also popular across this tiny state. Being a former territory of Portugal, Goa has a dominant western musical scene with the use of instrument such as the violin, drums, guitar, trumpet and piano. It has also produced a number of prominent musicians and singers for the world of Indian music. Portuguese Fado also has significance in Goa.

Lorna Cordeiro is a popular singer and is referred to as the *"nightingale of Goa"*. She sings in both English and Konkani. Some of her popular oldies are *Pisso, Bebdo, Red Rose, Tuzo mog* and *Noxibak Rodta.* Other popular musicians and singers include Anthony Gonsalves (violinist), António Fortunato de Figueiredo (conductor and violinist), Chris Perry(often called the king of Goan music), Hema Sardesai (playback singer), Ian D'Sa, (former guitarist of Canadian band Billy Talent, of Goan descent), Remo Fernandes (musician and playback singer), Kishori Amonkar (classical vocalist), Dinanath Mangeshkar (dramatist and classical vocalist), and Oliver Sean (singer/ songwriter). Goa has produced many performers of Indian classical music, such as the vocalist Kesarbai Kerkar, Lata Mangeshkar and Asha Bhosle.

Goan local bands are also known for their use of western music styles and are popular at both, public and private celebrations. Goa has become home to a style of Electronic music, the Trance music. It is popular at the Electronic music festivals hosted yearly in Goa that attract people from over 50 countries. However, owing to the tourism peak around the Christmas-New year period, the festivals have either been cancelled or rescheduled on other dates.

Traditional music

The traditional Goan musical instruments include *dhol, mridanga, tabla, ghumat, dholak, kasale, madlem, shehnai, surt, tasso, nagado,* and *tambura.* The ghumat is an earthenware pot-like vessel made by Goan potters with openings on the two opposite sides, one large and the other small in diameter, with the middle portion much bulging outwards. On the larger opening with the edge conveniently moulded for the fitting, a wet skin of a lizard (lacerta ocelata), known in Konkani as sap or gar, is fully stretched to cover the whole surface of the opening. The ghumat is essential for Hindu festivals, some temple rituals like Suvari vadan, bhivari and mando performances.

A madlem is a cylindrical earthen vessel covered at both ends with the skin of a lizard and is mostly played by the Kunbis.

Being part of Portugal for over 450 years led to the introduction of the piano, mandolin and violin to Goa. Other instruments such as the drums, guitar and trumpet were also widely used. Schools in this period taught pupils at least one such instrument. It is said that *Goans have music in their blood*, a statement further strengthened by the role music and dance plays in Goan culture. Popular folk dances such as the Portuguese Corridinho are still part of Catholic weddings.

Konkani song may be classified in four groups: one which draws on the more pristine form in music and verse, as in the *fugdi* or the *dhalo*; the second which blends western and native music but retains Konkani lyrics as in deknnis; the third which blends native and western music as well as language as in dulpod; and the fourth which has a marked influence of western music and lyrics (in Konkani) with borrowed Portuguese words as in mando.

As many as 35 types of Konkani Song have been classified. These include *banvarh, deknni, dhalo, dulpod, duvalo, fell* song, *fughri, kunnbi* song, *launimm, mando, ovi, palnnam, talghari, tiatr* song, *zagor* song and *zoti.* The Christian hymns and Hindu religious songs are also characterized separately with the former related to contemporary western styles.

- Banvarh is a mourning song, usually sung on the day of cremation by Hindus.
- Deknni is a song which originated in Bardez, Ilhas and Salcete.
- Dhalo is a wedding song.
- Dulpod is a dance song with quick rhythm and themes from everyday Goan life.
- Duvallo is a pregnancy song.
- Fell is folk drama with themes from Indian epics or Indian history. It is performed by wandering artists usually after the rains, which start in June and end in August or September. The *fell* song is a dance song.

- Fughri is a dance song performed on religious occasions, particularly in honour of the deity Ganesha.
- The *Kunnbi*, who are probably together with the *Gaudde* the oldest inhabitants of Goa, belong to the peasant strata. The kunnbi song is a dance song in the fughri style depicting their own life, but also protesting against exploitation and social discrimination in a subtle manner.
- Launim is a song dealing with religious and legendary themes.
- Mando is a dance song whose major theme is love, the minor ones being historical narratives, grievance against exploitation and social injustice, and political resistance during the Portuguese presence in Goa.
- Ovi, which the Portuguese termed as versos, is a song with nuptial themes. It has the Sanskrit root *vri* which means "to choose, to select". The ovi has three rhymed lines and one unrhymed. The former contain each three or four words and the fourth line one, two, and exceptionally three words. The number of syllables is nine for the rhymed lines and four or five for the last line. The early Portuguese Christian missionaries adopted the ovi-form for liturgical and devotional hymns.
- Palnnam is a cradle song, a lullaby.
- Talgarhi is a song of the Gaudde. The theatre song is sung during the stage play, mainly performed by wandering artists during the dry season. They entertain the public while touching on daily life, but also sing subtle satires on local politics and the shortcomings of Goans.
- Zagor means "watch". The zagor song is sung in kunnbi folk plays depicting their own life. They are usually staged at night. * Zoti is sung at nuptials.

The Christian hymns and Hindu songs for the liturgy and popular devotions form an essential part of Goan daily life. It is common for passersby to hear people playing instruments in their houses during the evening hours.

Western, Portuguese and indigenous

Goa, a part of India since 1961, had been part of Portugal for over 450 years and hence has closer connections with Western classical and popular music. Use of Portuguese music and other western music is popular specifically at most Catholic weddings and celebrations. Live bands are a celebratory feature at such weddings and are generally clubbed with a local Disc Jockey to allow for intervals to be covered also.

Over the centuries, indigenous Goan music was blended with European music, particularly that of Portugal. Hence Goan music uses western styles, notes and musical instruments more significantly than regional Asian variants. The Goa Symphony Orchestra and Goa Philharmonic Choir were founded by Lourdino Barreto.

Another major attraction of the Goan music industry is the *Tiatr* derived from the Portuguese word *'teatro'* meaning *theater*. It is a type of musical theatre still very popular with Goans, resident in Goa or Bombay as well as with expatriates and resident communities in the Middle East, London and other major western cities (where Konkani speakers have a considerable presence). The dramas are performed in the Roman Konkani dialects and include music, dancing and singing. Tiatr performers are called *tiatrists*. Songs integral to the plays are known as 'Kants'. Other songs, called *kantaram* are generally either comedic or based on topical, political and controversial issues that are interspersed through the performance. These musical interludes are independent of the main theme of the play. The songs are often satirical and unsparing of the politics and politicians of Goa. The music is provided by a live band including keyboard, trumpet, saxophone, bass guitar and drums. This century old theater industry in Goa still remains independent of government control and efforts to bring it under such control have met massive opposition from locals for fear of government regulation over content of political nature.

The Monte Music Festival hosted by Lisbon-headquartered Fundação Oriente, in partnership with the hotel Cidade de Goa is one of the premier cultural events on Goa's crowded calendar. Every year, the three-day concert features both Indian and Western classical music along with dance performances held at the spectacularly situated Capela do Monte, high above the old capital of the Estado da India (former Portuguese state). The area is a UNESCO world heritage site.

The recently introduced annual two-day Ketevan World Sacred music festival offers music programs, courses and conferences with artists from several traditions around the world including Carnatic, Christian, Sufi, Hindustani, Jewish, Orthodox and many others. Artists like Santiango Girelli (orchestra conductor from Argentina), Rocio De Frutos (soprano from Spain) and Leo Rossi (violinist from Argentina) have participated in past events.

Konkani liturgical music and choirs

Goa has a rich heritage of Konkani liturgical music and hymns. The standard hymnal of the Archdiocese of Goa and Daman is called *Gaionancho Jhelo* (Garland of hymns) and the diocese also brings out a periodical sheet music publication of Konkani liturgical hymns a called *Devacheam Bhurgeanchim Gitam* (Songs of God's children).

As with the liturgy, the entire music of the Catholic church in Goa is in the Latin script.

Churches across Goa always maintain choirs. Like most Catholic churches worldwide, there are separate choirs for adults and children. Some historically significant seminaries also maintain choirs of their own. A notable one is the all-male seminarians of the *Santa Cecilia Choir* (Coro di Santa Cecilia), part of the over 400 year old Rachol seminary (*Seminário de Rachol)* of Goa.The choir has also been known to use a 16th-century restored pipe organ for its concerts. Most of the centuries-old churches in Goa feature these pipe organs, but few are known to use them now because of their upkeep. However, they still form part of the churches interior decor and in almost all instances are located in the nave above the main entrances facing the altar in the far end below.

Pop

In the area of Western music, there are several pop stars, among them Remo Fernandes (born 1953). Goan popular music is generally sung in the Konkani language and English language. Another contributor to Goan music is the Canadian-Goan band Goa Amigos, which has represented Goa at the largest South Asian festival in North America.

Home for electronic music

Goa has become a home for electronic music, especially a style called Goa trance. This genre began its evolution in the late 1960s, when hippies from the United States, United Kingdom and elsewhere turned Goa into a tourist destination. When tourism began to die out, a number of devotees stayed in the area, pursuing a specific style of trance music. Early pioneers included Mark Allen, Goa Gil and Fred Disko.

Goa trance

Goa Trance (sometimes referred to as Goa or by the number 604) is a form of electronic music that developed around the same time as Trance music became popular in Europe. It originated during the late 1980s and early 1990s in the Indian state of Goa. Essentially, Trance music was pop culture's answer to the Goa Trance music scene on the beaches of Goa where the traveler's music scene has been famous since the time of the Beatles. Goa Trance enjoyed the greater part of its success from around 1994 -1998, and since then has dwindled significantly both in production and consumption, being replaced by its successor, Psychedelic Trance (also known as psytrance). Many of the original Goa Trance artists: Hallucinogen, Slinky Wizard, and Total Eclipse are still making music, but refer to their style of music simply as "PSY". TIP Records, Flying Rhino Records, Dragonfly Records, Transient Records, Phantasm Records, Symbiosis Records, Blue Room Released were all key players on the beach and in the scene.

Goa Trance is closely related to the emergence of Psytrance

during the latter half of the 1990s and early 2000s, where the two genres mixed together. In popular culture, the distinction between the two genres often remains largely a matter of opinion (they are considered by some to be synonymous; others say that Psytrance is more "psychedelic/cybernetic" and that Goa Trance is more "organic", and still others maintain that there is a clear difference between the two). If anything, the styles are easier to differentiate in Central and Eastern Europe (e.g. Austria, Hungary, Romania) where Goa Trance parties are more popular than Psy-Trance parties - the opposite being true in the UK, Belgium and Germany. Psy Trance has a noticeably more aggressive bass line and Goa tends to avoid the triplet-style bass lines. Between them however, both psy- and Goa trance are sonically distinct from other forms of trance in both tonal quality, structure and feel. In many countries they are generally more underground and less commercial than other forms of trance, except for Brazil and Israel, which since the year of 2000 it became both countries most popular type of music for the general party scene. Top DJ's from the UK and other parts of Western Europe fly to Goa for special parties, often on the beaches or in rice paddies. "*Shorebar*" at Anjuna Beach in Northern Goa is traditionally seen as the birthplace and center of the Goan trance scene.

MEDIA AND COMMUNICATION

Goa is served by almost all television channels available in India. Channels are received through cable in most parts of Goa. In the interior regions, channels are received via satellite dishes. Doordarshan, the national television broadcaster, has two free terrestrial channels on air.

DTH (Direct To Home) TV services are available from Dish TV, Videocon D2H, Tata Sky & DD Direct Plus. The All India Radio is the only radio channel in the state that broadcasts on both FM and AM bands. Two AM channels are broadcast, the primary channel at 1287 kHz and the Vividh Bharati channel at 1539 kHz. AIR's FM channel is called FM Rainbow and is broadcast at 105.4 MHz. A number of private FM radio channels are available, Big FM at 92.7 and Radio Indigo at 91.9 MHz. There is also an educational radio channel, Gyan Vani, run by IGNOU broadcast from Panaji at 107.8 MHz. In 2006, St Xavier's College, Mapusa, became the first college in the state to launch a campus community radio station "Voice of Xavier's".

Major cellular service operators include Bharti Airtel, Vodafone Essar, Idea Cellular, Telenor, Reliance Infocomm, Tata DoCoMo, BSNL CellOne and Jio.

Local publications include the English language *O Heraldo* (Goa's oldest, once a Portuguese language paper), *The Gomantak Times* and *The Navhind Times*. In addition to these, *The Times of India* and *The Indian Express* are also received from Mumbai and Bangalore in the urban areas. *The Times of India* has recently started publication from Goa itself, serving the local population news directly from the state capital. Among the list of officially accredited newspapers are *O Heraldo*, *The Navhind Times* and *The Gomantak Times* in English; *Bhaangar Bhuin* in Konkani (Devanagari script); and *Tarun Bharat*, *Gomantak*, *Navprabha*, *Goa Times*, *Sanatan Prabhat*, *Govadoot* and *Lokmat* (all in Marathi). All are dailies. Other publications in the state include *Planet Goa* (English, monthly), *Goa Today* (English, monthly), *Goan Observer* (English, weekly), *Vauraddeancho Ixtt* (Roman-script Konkani, weekly) *Goa Messenger*, *Vasco Watch*, *Gulab* (Konkani, monthly), *Bimb* (Devanagari-script Konkani).

THE BANGLE WEARING CEREMONY

The bangle wearing ceremony that is held once in her life time for the bride to be is called the Chuddo. The bangles symbolise married life for the bride, as they are broken only on her dead husband's coffin.

The Chuddo among the upper castes, consists of a set of seven glass bangles of a green colour on each wrist. Among the lower castes, the bangles are of the seven colours of rainbow. This ceremony is performed on the eve of marriage or a day or two days before. It is done at the house of the maternal uncle of the bride. In the normal case, these bangles are put on her, by the bangle seller.

Other relatives and those present at the ceremony are also given by him a pair or more of their choice free of cost. There are songs sung during this time which are typical and appropriate to the occasion. Offerings of money in token of blessing are put in a tray placed before the bangle seller. The money collected thus is taken by him over and above the payment that he gets for the work done.

There are women who are experts in singing in parables and pointed metaphor in the form of Zotis as well as throwing aside all taunts to them and other home people, *i.e.* relatives and would be relatives.

After this ceremony at the maternal uncles house, the said uncle sends his niece home with a vojem (a parcel of sweet-meats in a big special type of bamboo woven basket) containing sweet meats, bananas, bread- twelve each in number. This system is known as Perkund.

Similar Perkund calls without the festive bangle are made, when other relatives invite her at their place for lunch or dinner of farewell.

She receives a special bunch of flowers from her uncle and others on this occasion. Even if the parents of the bride, do not happen to be on speaking terms with the said uncle or relatives, she has to go and get at least water from their well. If they have no well or it is not possible to get water from there, then some water has to be taken from their house by the bride.

Relatives visit the two houses of the bride and of the groom, with flowers etc. Special 'fole' cakes made of rice-flour stuffed with shredded coconut mixed with jaggery, cupped into a wrapping of jack-fruit tree leaves and pinned by a thin stick-pin are served at the maternal uncle's house.

Or it may be 'mankeo' some thing like dosas stuffed with coconut-shredding and jaggery. The Chuddo ceremony is same for both Hindus and Muslims. The 'Saddo' a variant of the saree is a special dress, usually flowery or plain red or pink, worn by the bride in the house, at the day of the wedding after the official function is over.

It is given by the maternal uncle to the bride among Hindus and Christians. Among Muslims no such practice is noticed.

SADDO CEREMONY

In the northern part of Goa, there is a beautiful ceremony called the Saddo. Saddo is the ceremonial cutting of the cloth, normally flowery red, to be worn by the bride in the house after the wedding. A tiny image of child Jesus is placed on the floor mat where the tailor is sitting with the clothes, at their house and two tiny length wise pieces of clothes are cut by him and placed there in the form of a cross.

To begin with, there is the 'Nomon' in which blessing of God almighty and especially of the virgin Mary, mother of Jesus are invoked in the form of Zot (a special song peculiar to the occasion sung by an expert song-stress). Then each relative, from the nearest to begin with, followed by others to the accompaniment of references to them made in beautiful metaphor in the form of Zotis, walks up to the spot where lies the Infant Jesus and lays his or her offerings of money from Rs2 to Rs10 before the image.

Then a piece of betel nut and leaf with calcined lime and some sweets are disturbed to the people present. The elder men are served with liquor, women and children with sweet red wine and soft drinks.

The money collected on the occasion is taken by the tailor, apart from his wages.

The tailor will later stitch the main wedding dress or gown in milky white colour and other necessary clothes for the bride and near relatives, brides maids etc. The brides gown, ornaments and trousseau are displayed in a special ceremony at which people are invited, and then they are sent to the groom's place for display there.

THE HAIR CUTTING RITUAL

On the day prior to the marriage, the groom is set on a ceremonial stool or chair at home and the barber formerly the family barber, cuts his hair in an appropriate cut. Songs are sung on the occasion and friends and relatives gather to witness it. The barber is paid a handsome remuneration in cash as well as given presents in the form of coconut and a measure of rice and sweet meats. This ceremony is held prior to the bath with coconut-pulp, juice or milk. This ceremony is held among all communities.

The bath with coconut pulp: Among Christians, on the evening preceding the wedding day the bride at her place and the groom at his, take a ceremonial bath with coconut pulp-juice or milk. It starts with applying ceremonially to the accompaniment of special verses called Zotis, peculiar to the occasion, sung by trained women. On the head or a part of the body of the bride or groom, clad in bathing dress, at his /her own place, a tumbler full or cup full of juice extracted from coconut-shredded pulp kept in a pot is applied, by relatives in a proper order of priority, followed by friends. This is done first, out side the bathing room, in the hall.

The second part of the bathing ceremony consists of a bath with water possibly warm in the bathing room, again in a ceremonial manner, with songs being sung in a group. After bathing with a tumbler of water, a few coins are dropped into the pot of water, kept for the purpose. All the money dropped into the pots is taken by the maids who helped or were called for preparing the bath water and coconut pulp juice.

Hindus too have a similar bath but not so elaborate. They have an additional application of turmeric (halad) and oil on the body of the bride. Among Muslims, this practice does not exist.

THE BEGGAR'S LUNCH

Among Christians, a lavish feast called the Beggar's lunch or Bhick Reamfevon is held a day or two before the wedding day, preferably on a Tuesday. Seven or nine poor people, both men and women are invited to a sumptuous lunch with pork, beef, fish, rice and a curry of a special type called 'samrachi koddi'. They squat on the floor mat and specially prepared jack fruit tree leaves, well plaited into plates, are placed before them into which food is served or ladled out by the bride and groom at each one's place of residence.

The intention behind the service is to feed and satisfy the ancestors on this important occasion in their house through the medium of these beggars. Coconut oil is also given for their hair and a bidi or cigarette, according to the preference expressed by them. They are also given a sweet dish of gram dal and soji a sweet composed of wheat preparation and bananas. Instead of coconut-feni, a sweet wine could also be served to them.

WEDDING CEREMONY

Wedding in Goa do not take place on Thursdays and Fridays in the normal course. On the wedding day, the groom's sister and another close relative go with the brides dress and assorted materials and dress her up at her residence. The wedding ceremony of Goa is same as all over the world. There will be a wedding dance function in the hall. After the dance function is over, the whole group or part of it that remains to the end.

The groom's side cross over a line of demarcation, imaginary but conventionally drawn called 'shim' (literally, boundary line in Konkani), the brides guests remaining on the hither side of the boundary. The boundary being normally the place where the roads going towards the residence of the parties, part from each other in a fork. Here a prayer is said and wishes expressed for the prosperity and happiness of the married couple. Some liquor from a bottle brought by the grooms or bride's people, is taken in little cupfuls by those present and without crossing the boundary line.

At this time of pouring the liquor the shim should not be crossed, until this brief ritual is over. Later one or two relatives from the bride's side come and cross the 'shim', to formally invite the bridal couple to the bride's place which in Konkani is called 'Apovnnem' (invitation) for the return of the couple on the next day for what is known as the Portovnnem (ceremonial return). This practice of pouring the liquor and observing the shim is being given up now.

Among the Hindus, at both houses the priest is called and he performs the 'punnyavaham' and 'nandhishradha' readings in the presence of the groom/bride and their parents. Then oil and turmeric is applied after which they take bath from a barrel of water placed there for the purpose. Married women with husbands living (sovashnni) go with oil and turmeric from bride to groom and from groom to bride. The wedding ritual is held at the bride's place where the maternal uncle takes the lead in the ceremonies. At the groom's place, the groom's married sister ties the wedding turban called the bashing.

Then the marriage procession sets out, with the sister of the groom carrying with herself, a pot with leaves of mango on which is placed a coconut. Another sister carries a wicker basket with a lighted lamp. They are followed by the groom in his full regalia. He is received at the bride's place ceremonially and led into the marriage chamber where the religious ceremony is performed by the priest.

Among the Christians, the day following that of the wedding, at the groom's place there is a brief ceremony of wearing the bangles at the home by the bangle-vendor of the village. They are put on the wrist of the bride. The vendor is later given a coconut, a measure of rice and payment in cash for his services.

At the groom's place, in the morning following the wedding day, a session of ceremonial blessing in kind is held. In that session, close relatives, from the mother-in-law of the bride on wards give presents normally in the form of gold ornaments to her. This was being done earlier, to the accompaniment of songs, verses and prayers.

Later around lunch, the bride and groom with a small retinue of close relatives go to the brides place. They are received at the bride's place and there may be a dance or simply a litany (ladin) in thanks giving and a small get together and service of drinks and food.

At the bride's place in Goa, at this time there is also the 'folle-fevonn' a sumptuous luncheon for close relatives. After this luncheon, the bride and groom among the upper class, used to go, sitting in a machila (palanquin) led by boias (bearers) along with a red coloured rush-mat or floor-mat with a 'vojem', a parcel of sweet meats, bananas etc. to accompany them to the groom's place of residence.

Among the Sudras, on the day following the wedding day, a group of masked friends from the groom's side comes to the bride's place along with their retinue. They sing songs and wash the feet of the bridal couple who tip them liberally. A ceremony called 'Tollvar' sitting was held consisting of kurponn (mat of bamboo placed on the pot of rice while draining water from it) and turbaned men would approach the married couple with salt and chillies and say some incantations so as to take away the evil eye from the couple. After this they went through the movements of shaving the bride groom. There was another Tollvar sitting at the bride's place at the time of the return of the bride to her place in the Portovnnem (ceremonial return). Among the Hindus, after the bride becomes a part of the grooms household by virtue of her marriage to him, a ceremony is held to welcome her into the fold of his (husband's) gotra, in a ritual called Gotraint haddop.

The bride has to show a lit lamp before eight people, all from the groom's side. She has also to offer them ghee, bananas and snacks. Before leaving for the groom's place, five couples along with the bride and the groom are seated and rice is thrown on them in a ceremony called 'Sensorbhorp'.

Among the Christians, all the elders of the house gave ornaments or cash as presents to the new son-in-law. The girl would be given things necessary to set up her new household like mattresses, pillows etc. After the marriage ceremony is over, the groom with his bride has to sit on the mattress and get himself acquainted with all the elders of his in- laws. The bride's handicrafts, trousseau, jewel box etc. would then be displayed for all to see and then sent to her in-laws.

After the ghar-pravesh (entry of the bride to the groom's house) there used to be a programme of giving a fresh name to the new bride. The groom had to write the proposed name for the bride by his own fingers in the rice grains from a stand proffered to him. Such a practice is on the wane now.

FAMILY ORGANISATION

The concept of marriage as a sacrament and that too monogamous in nature is very much the norm among both the Hindus and Christian in Goa. It is a social contract among the Muslims. In Goa, the family organisation is basically elementary or nuclear in character. The break-up and separate residence for the new couple may begin after the marriage of the subsequent sons. The other sons staying outside in a nuclear family of their own are called virilocal. When one of the son continues to stay with his new family in his father's house after his marriage, the household is called patrilocal.

Parents in their old age may take up residence with one of their married sons. Ghor-zanvoim is the case in which the son-in-law of the house, who resides matrilocally, being adopted into the house of his in-laws in the event of his marrying the daughter of the house, if she is the only child or the one chosen for such an alliance. For any important decision to be taken in the interest of the family in the matter of education of a higher nature or a marriage alliance, all the members advise and come or rather cooperate to bring into fruition.

Respect for the elders is very strong in all the communities. The eldest male of the family, generally the father, is the head of the family and in his absence, the mother officiates in that position.

SPORTS

Normally other states are fond of cricket but association

football is the most popular sport in Goa and is embedded in Goan culture as a result of the Portuguese influence. Its origins in the state are traced back to 1883 when the visiting Irish priest Fr. William Robert Lyons established the sport as part of a "Christian education". On 22 December 1959 the *Associação de Futebol de Goa* was formed, which continues to administer the game in the state under the new name Goa Football Association. Goa, along with West Bengal and Keralais the locus of football in India and is home to many football clubs in the national I-League. The state's football powerhouses include Salgaocar, Dempo, Churchill Brothers, Vasco, Sporting Clube de Goa and FC Goa. The first Unity World Cup was held in Goa in 2014. The state's main football stadium, Fatorda Stadium, is located at Margao and also hosts cricket matches. The state hosted few matches of the 2017 FIFA U-17 World Cup in Fatorda Stadium.

Fatorda Stadium

A number of Goans have represented India in football and six of them, namely Samir Naik, Climax Lawrence, Brahmanand

Sankhwalkar, Bruno Coutinho, Mauricio Afonso and Roberto Fernandes have all captained the national team. Goa has its own state football team and league, the Goa Professional League. It is probably the only state in India where cricket is not considered the most important of all sports.

Goa also has its own cricket team. Dilip Sardesai remains the only Goan to date to play international cricket for India.

The Indian Olympic Association (IOA) has won the right to host the Asian Beach Games in 2020.

3

Government and Politics

GOVERNMENT OF GOA

The Government of Goa is the provincial government created by Constitution of India as executive, legislative and judicial authority of state of Goa. It is located in Panaji, Goa.

History

The governor's role is largely ceremonial, but plays a crucial role when it comes to deciding who should form the next government or in suspending the legislature as has happened in the recent past. After having stable governance for nearly thirty years up to 1990, Goa is now notorious for its political instability having seen fourteen governments in the span of the fifteen years between 1990 and 2005. In March 2005 the assembly was dissolved by the governor and President's Rule was declared, which suspended the legislature. A by-election in June 2005 saw the Congress coming back to power after winning three of the five seats that went to polls. The Congress party and the Bharatiya Janata Party (BJP) are the two largest parties in the state. In the assembly pole of 2007, Congress-led coalition won and started ruling the state. Other parties include the United Goans Democratic Party, the Nationalist

Congress Party and the Maharashtrawadi Gomantak Party. In the 2012 election the Bharatiya Janata Party (BJP) defeated the Indian National Congress government in Goa, led by Chief Minister Digambar Kamat. The election was won by the BJP-Maharashtrawadi Gomantak alliance which won 24 seats in the 40-seat assembly. The Bharatiya Janata Party won 21 seats, while the Maharashtrawadi Gomantak Party won 3 seats. Manohar Parrikar, leader of the BJP, was sworn in as Chief Minister of Goa on 9 March 2012.

GOVERNMENT AND POLITICS IN GOA

Goa Assembly

The politics of Goa are a result of the uniqueness of this region due to 450 years of Portuguese rule, in comparison to three centuries of British colonialism experienced by the rest of India. The Indian National Congress was unable to achieve electoral success in the first two decades after the State's incorporation into India. Instead, the state was dominated by the regional political parties like Maharashtrawadi Gomantak Party and the United Goans Party.

Government

In the Parliament of India, Goa has two seats in the Lok Sabha (House of the People), one representing each district, and one seat in the Rajya Sabha (Council of the States).

Goa's administrative capital is Panaji in English, Pangim in Portuguese, and Ponjê in the local language. It lies on the left bank of the Mandovi. The seat of the Goa Legislative Assembly is in Porvorim, across the Mandovi from Panaji. As the state comes under the Bombay High Court, Panaji has a bench of it. Unlike other states, which follow the British Indian model of civil laws framed for individual religions, the Portuguese Goa Civil Code, a uniform code based on the Napoleonic code, has been retained in Goa.

Goa has a unicameral legislature of 40 members, headed by a speaker. The Chief Minister heads the executive, which is made up from the party or coalition elected with a majority in the legislature. The Governor, the head of the state, is appointed by the President of India. After having stable governance for nearly thirty years up to 1990, Goa is now notorious for its political instability having seen fourteen governments in the span of the fifteen years between 1990 and 2005. In March 2005 the assembly was dissolved by the Governor and President's Rule was declared, which suspended the legislature. A by-election in June 2005 saw the Indian National Congress coming back to power after winning three of the five seats that went to polls. The Congress Party and the Bharatiya Janata Party (BJP) are the two largest parties in the state. In the assembly poll of 2007, the INC-led coalition won and formed the government. In the 2012 Vidhan Sabha Elections, the Bharatiya Janata Party along with the Maharashtrawadi Gomantak Party won a clear majority, forming the new government with Manohar Parrikar as the Chief Minister. Other parties include the United Goans Democratic Party, the Nationalist Congress Party. In the 2017 assembly elections, the Indian National Congress gained the most seats, with the BJP coming in second. However, no party was able to gain a majority in the 40 member house. The BJP was invited to form the Government by Governor Mridula Sinha. The Congress claimed the use of money power on the part of the BJP and took the case to the Supreme Court. However, the Manohar Parikkar led Government was able to prove its majority in the Supreme Court mandated "floor test".

UNITED GOANS PARTY

The United Goans Party is a political party in Goa.

UGP was founded after its annexation into India. Its main aim at the time of formation was to protect the distinct identity of Goa and the Goan people. The UGP played a critical role in persuading the government of India to hold a referendum on the issue of Goa's merger with Maharashtra.

Formation

After Goa's annexation into the Indian union in 1961, Goa became a union territory with its own legislature. Elections to the state assembly were scheduled to be held in 1963. There were calls from many sections in Goa and the neighbouring state of Maharashtra to merger the tiny state into Maharashtra. This demand was spearheaded by the Maharashtrawadi Gomantak Party.

Sensing that the merger would mean the gradual disappearing of Goa's distinct identity and culture, four parties merged to form the United Goans Party in September 1963. The four parties were the Partido Indiano, Goan National Union, United Front Goans and Goancho Paksh. Its first president was Dr. Jack de Sequeira. The United Goans Party was formed by merging Goencho Pokx of Jack Sequeira, the Partido Indiano of Alvaro Loyola de Furtado, the Goa National union of J M Desouza and United Fronts of Goans and Democratic Party who shared a common goal, that of separate identity for Goa, and which was against the merger of Goa with Maharashtra. The think tank for the United Goans Party came from its second in command, Dr. Loyola Furtado, who many consider as the brains behind the United Goans Party. The main support base for the UGP came from the Catholics of Goa and upper-caste Hindus. Although it was predominantly Christian it did not exclude other groups and also put up Hindu and Muslim candidates.

Performance in Elections

In the first elections held in 1963, the MGP secured 16 from a total of 30. UGP put up candidates in 24 constituencies and secured 12 and formed the opposition. Two seats, one from

Daman and Diu each went to independent candidates. De Sequeira became the leader of the Opposition. Its main manifesto item was "Separate Statehood in and outside the Assembly of the Union Territory of Goa, Daman and Diu and in Parliament". Among its key promises were the setting up of a University, industrialization, land reforms and the recognition of Konkani as the regional language.

The Church supported the Catholic-dominated UGP against the Communist-led Frente Popular.

Role in the Goa Opinion Poll

Following MGPs victory in the first election, the MGP demanded that Goa be merged into Maharashtra. The MGP wanted that the issue should be voted in the Goa legislature, as was the norm in a representative democracy. The UGP was of the opinion that such an important decision should not be left to them MLAs but should be put before the people of Goa to decide. If the merger was to be voted in the Goa legislature, it was a foregone conclusion that the MGP with its majority would push through the merger.

The MGP MLAs visited New Delhi several times to convince them to hold a referendum in Goa. First they met Jawaharlal Nehru; and after his death, met Lal Bahadur Shastri to press for a referendum.

However Shastri died in 1966 in Tashkent and this decision was now left to the new Prime Minister Indira Gandhi. The UGP delegation met her and submitted a memorandum that such a monumental decision affecting the future of the State could not be left to legislators alone, but should be put before the people to decide. Finally the central government agreed to hold a referendum in Goa.

The UGP demanded that all people from Goa, regardless of where they were staying in India, should be allowed to vote. Those staying outside Goa could vote by postal ballot. However this request was denied. They also demanded that all deputationinsts from Maharashtra should not be allowed to vote and that the Bandodkar ministry should resign to conduct a free and fair poll. The centre conceded the demand for Bandodkar's resignation.

The opinion poll was held on 16 January 1967. A total of 3,17,633 votes were polled. The merger was defeated by 34,021 votes.

First Split

A section of UGP MLAs were unhappy with the very idea of an Opinion Poll. A splinter group of four MLAs headed by Dr. Alvaro De Loyala Furtado came to be known as United Goans (Furtado Group). The main body of the party was known as United Goans (Sequeira Group). The U.G.(F) received recognition from the Election Commission and used *The Rising Sun* as its symbol.

The Furtado Group received the support from Goa Organised Alliance and fielded eight candidates in the next election. The Sequeira Group used *The Hand* as a symbol. The symbol was associated with St. Francis Xavier. It contested all thirty seats this time, claiming primary responsibility for the Opinion Poll and its verdict and promised a *separate Konkani State of Goa.*

Second Split

In 1977, Erasmo de Sequeira joined hands with the Bharatiya Lok Dal, headed by Charan Singh. He did this without consulting his party members. The party members were enraged, causing the UGP(Sequeira group) to split into two groups: UGP (Sequeria Group) and UGP (Naik Group). He lost the next parliamentary election to Eduardo Faleiro of UGP-N in March 1977. In the next Assembly elections, UGP-S managed to win just three seats as compared to UGP-N, which won 10 seats.

Decline

The UGP had never won an election. It split, first in 1967 and the second time in 1977. Its decline (1977–1989) corresponded with the rise of the Congress, a national party which did not win any seat in the first elections. Finally it merged with the Congress.

Revival in 2016

In 2016 December, former Minister Babush Monteserrate revived United Goans Party.

MAHARASHTRAWADI GOMANTAK PARTY

Maharashtrawadi Gomantak Party (MGP) was Goa's first ruling party after the end of Portuguese colonial rule in 1961. In the first elections held after India took over the former Portuguese colony, it ascended to power in December 1963 and stayed on, till being ousted from power by defections in early 1979.

The party has its base amongst non-Brahmin Hindus, a group that make up a large section of the poorer half of the Goan society, and was particularly deprived during Portuguese rule in Goa. It held on to power despite being affected by some defections, for much of the first two decades of post-Portuguese Goa, defeating the other contenders for power—primarily the United Goans Party not to be confused with the United Goans Democratic Party, founded in the 1990s first, and later the Congress.

History

MGP's first chief minister was the mine owner Dayanand Bandodkar, followed by his daughter, Shashikala Kakodkar, who ascended to power after her father died in office, approximately a decade after taking over power, in 1973.

After Shashikala Kakodkar left MGP and joined Congress, Ramakant Khalap became leader of MGP in Goa Assembly and from just two seats under his charismatic leadership MGP won 18 seats in the subsequent elections. As recorded by the Supreme Court of India in the cases Dr. Kashinath Jalmi vs State of Goa and Ravi NaikV/s State of Goa at one time MGP had clear majority of 25 MLAs in the 40-member Assembly of Goa, however by blatant misuse of his powers under the Anti Defection Law and Constitution of India, the then Governor of Goa did not make Khalap Chief Minister of Goa.

MGP's plank was largely based on populism, and promising a better deal to the Hindu economically deprived and socially oppressed sections in Goa. It was initially associated with a plank of merging Goa with the neighbouring state of Maharashtra, a policy it subsequently backed away from when the 1967 Opinion Poll held in the region voted against the merger. It has also supported the use of the Marathi language; though some interpret its stand on language and merger as being partly a means of fighting caste issues and countering the domination of Goa by the traditional Hindu and Catholic elites.

During the first 18 years after integration with independent India, MGP led the state government. Today, however, the MGP is marginalized when compared to its former status. The Bharatiya Janata Party (BJP), particularly during its reign between 1999 and 2005, was showing increasing signs of having taken over most of the Hindu voters, and a large chunk of the party cadre.

The BJP allied with the MGP in the elections of 1994, and made inroads into that party's vote-base, even though it won only four seats in that election, and the MGP got 10. Over the years, the MGP, which is symbolized by a lion and has a saffron flag, has been further eroded by the ascendent BJP. The crisis had even reached the point where dissolution of the party was discussed. Although the MGP has been part of the BJP-led National Democratic Alliance, the MGP and the BJP have been experiencing a rift to where Dhavalikar demanded that Laxmikant Parsekar (BJP) should resign as chief minister of Goa as a precondition for alliance talks for the 2017 polls. Parsekar responded by saying that the MGP's MLAs should resign if they were not satisfied with the CM.

Following an election in the early 2000s, the MGP were reduced to just one seat (out of a total of 40 seats) in the Goa legislative assembly, while the BJP made large gains.

In the Lok Sabha parliamentary elections of 2004, the party had launched candidates in both constituencies in Goa. They got 5377 and 2207 votes.

Deepak Dhavlikar who is also the honorable minister for cooperation is the president of the party and Lavoo S. Mamledar is the general secretary.

1994 - 1999

In the early 1990s, the BJP was steadily gaining strength in national politics and was emerging as an alternative to the Indian National Congress (INC) at the Center. Hoping to end years of Congress rule in the state, the MGP entered into a pre-poll alliance with the BJP in Goa.

Considering that the MGP drew its support from the Bahujan Samaj and the BJP's demands for the demolition of the Babri Masjid, many believed that the electoral alliance would prove to be a tough competition to the ruling Congress as it would help consolidate the majority Hindu votes in its favor.

The MGP contested 25 seats whereas the BJP fielded its candidates from 12 constituencies. However, in the state elections, the Congress emerged as the single largest party, yet again, winning 18 seats. The MGP received 12 whereas 4 BJP legislators were also elected. The candidates who won the elections on MGP ticket in 1994 were:

Constituency	Candidate	Gender
Pernem	Parshuram Kotkar	M
Dargalim (SC)	Deu Mandrekar	M
Mapusa	Surendra Shirsat	M
Siolim	Chandrakant Chodankar	M
Maem	Shashikala Kakodkar	F
Pale	Sadanand Malik	M
Ponda	Shivdas Atmaram Verekar	M
Priol	Dr. Kashinath Jalmi	M

Vasco-da-Gama	Menezes Mesquita	M
Savordem	Vishnu Prabhu	M
Quepem	Prakash Velip	M
Poiguinim	Govind Acharya	M

Following the results, the Congress formed a coalition government under the leadership of Pratapsinh Rane. However, in 1998, internal differences between the party leaders led to a split in the INC. Former CM Dr. Wilfred de Souza broke away with another 9 MLAs to form a new political party - the Goa Rajiv Congress which grabbed power, thanks to support extended by both, the MGP as well as the BJP. The government lasted for just 120 days and the INC seized power in November 1998, just a few months before the 1999 assembly polls.

The 1994 coalition with the BJP proved to be a strategic blunder for the MGP, affecting the prospects of the party in the future. The national party soon started eating into the MGP's traditional vote bank. As the BJP improved its tally over the next few elections, the MGP's strength has declined exponentially. Many of its top leaders and ordinary cadres have either shifted to other parties or retired from active politics. Since the 1994 assembly polls, the MGP's tally has never crossed the two digit mark.

1999 - 2002

In the 1999 elections to the state legislature, the MGP was reduced to a mere 4 seats. On the other hand, its former partner, the BJP increased its tally to 10. The INC won a simple majority by winning 21 seats and Luizinho Faleiro was sworn in as the Chief Minister.

Fearing internal rebellion, the Congress invited other parties to merge with it or join the government. A few days later, the United Goans Democratic Party merged into the ruling party increasing its strength to 23. Soon, even the MGP joined the government. The MGP legislators who won the 1999 polls are specified below:

Constituency	Candidate	Gender
Mandrem	Ramakant Dattaram Khalap	M
Bicholim	Pandurang Raut	M
Marcaim	Sudin Dhavalikar	M
Quepem	Prakash Velip	M

Assembly Elections 2007

The party improved its strength during the June 2007 state elections, in which it allied with the Indian National Congress party. The MGP got 9% of the vote and won two seats in the state assembly, a gain of one. The party entered a coalition government led by the Congress Party and also including the Nationalist Congress Party.

On 26 July 2007, its two MLAs and two Independent MLAs withdraw their support to Digambar Kamat Ministry leading to the reduction of his government into minority. However, they were later wooed back and the regime subsequently completed its full term.

Assembly Elections 2012

Prior to the elections to the state assembly in February 2012, the MGP withdrew its support to the Congress led coalition government citing the medium of instruction as one of the issues. It then entered into a pre-poll agreement with the BJP. Under this agreement, the party contested eight seats (Benaulim, Dabolim, Marcaim, Nuvem, Ponda, Priol, Quepem and Thivim) while its partner fielded its candidates in another 31 seats. The allies supported independent candidate Nirmala Sawant from Cumbharjua. The elections were important for the party as it had to win either 3 seats or over 95,000 votes to retain its electoral symbol.

The party won three seats, all in and around the city of Ponda in central Goa. The Dhavalikar brothers retained their seats - Deepak from Priol and Sudin from Marcaim. Meanwhile, the MGP candidate Lavoo Mamledar beat Congress heavyweight and incumbent Home Minister Ravi Naik. The BJP won another 21 seats. The BJP-MGP alliance came to power with the support of 26 MLAs including 2 independent candidates in the 40 member house. Sudinis the minister for PWD, Transport and River Navigation in the new cabinet. Deepak holds the portfolios of Co-operation, Factories & Boilers.

Assembly Elections 2017

Before 2017 Goa Legislative Assembly election, MGP broke the alliance with Bharatiya Janata Party. Later they joined hands with Goa Suraksha Manch of RSS leader Subhash Velingkar and Shiv Sena and contested of 27 seat in the state.

GOA LEGISLATIVE ASSEMBLY

The Goa Legislative Assembly is the unicameral legislature of the state of Goa in Western India. It consists of 40 members. In charge of the budget, the Assembly appropriates money for social programs, agricultural development, infrastructure development, etc. It is also responsible for proposing and levying taxes.

Following the end of Portuguese rule in 1961, Goa was placed under military administration headed by Lieutenant General Kunhiraman Palat Candeth as Lieutenant-Governor. But on 8 June 1962, military rule was replaced by civilian government when the Lieutenant-Governor nominated an informal Consultative Council of 29 nominated members to assist him in the administration of the territory. The first Council met on 24 September 1962 in a meeting open to the public.

The Assembly first convened on 9 January 1964 in the Secretariat building (Adil Shah's Palace). Hence, 9 January is marked as "Legislator's Day" every year in Goa. When Goa became a state of India in 1987, the number of seats in the Assembly was increased to 40.

Presently, the Assembly meets in its own Goa State Legislative Assembly Complex in Porvorim, Bardez. Construction on the building began on 22 January 1994, and its completion was inaugurated by Prime Minister Atal Bihari Vajpayee on 5 March 2000.

GOA CIVIL CODE

The Goa Civil Code, also called the Goa Family Law, is the set of civil laws that governs the residents of the Indian state of Goa. In India, as a whole, there are religion-specific civil codes that separately govern adherents of different religions. Goa is an exception to that rule, in that a single code governs all Goans, irrespective of religion, ethnicity or linguistic affiliation. The English translation of the civil code is available on the Government of Goa's e-Gazette dated 19-10-2018.

History

The Goa civil code is largely based on the Portuguese Civil Code (*Código Civil Português*) of 1867, which was introduced in Goa in 1870. Later, the code saw some modifications, based on:

- the Portuguese Gentile Hindu Usages Decrees of 1880 (*Código de usos e costumes dos hindus gentios de Goa*)
- the Portuguese Decrees on Marriage and Divorce of 1910 (*Lei do Divórcio: Decreto de 3 de Novembro de 1910*). After the establishment of the First Portuguese Republic, the civil code was liberalized to give women more freedom.
- the Portuguese Decrees on Canonical Marriages of 1946 (*Decreto 35.461: regula o casamento nas colónias portuguesas*)

The civil code was retained in Goa after its merger with the Indian Union in 1961, although in Portugal, the original Code was replaced by the new Portuguese Civil Code of 1966. In 1981, the Government of India appointed a Personal Law Committee to determine if the non-uniform laws of the Union could be extended to Goa. The Goa Muslim Shariah Organization supported the move, but it was met with stiff resistance from the Muslim Youth Welfare Association and the Goa Muslim Women's Associations.

Differences with the Indian law

Some ways in which the Goa Civil Code is different from other Indian laws include:

- A married couple jointly holds ownership of all the assets owned (before the marriage) or acquired (after the marriage) by each spouse. In case of a divorce, each spouse is entitled to a half share of the assets. However, the law also allows antenuptial agreements, which may state a different division of assets in case of a divorce. These agreements also allow the spouses to hold the assets acquired before marriage separately. Such agreements cannot be changed or revoked. A married person cannot sell the property without the consent of his/her spouse.
- The parents cannot disinherit their children entirely. At least half of their property has to be passed on to the children compulsorily. This inherited property must be shared equally among the children.
- Muslim men, who have their marriages registered in Goa, cannot practice polygamy. Also, there is no provision for a verbal divorce.

Uniformity

The Goa Civil Code is not strictly a uniform civil code, as it has specific provisions for certain communities. For example:

- The Hindu men have the right to bigamy under specific circumstances mentioned in *Codes of Usages and Customs of Gentile Hindus of Goa* (if the wife fails to deliver a child by the age of 25, or if she fails to deliver a male child by the age of 30). For other communities, the law prohibits bigamy.
- The Roman Catholics can solemnize their marriages in church after obtaining a No Objection Certificate from the Civil Registrar. For others, only a civil registration of the marriage is accepted as a proof of marriage. The

Catholics marrying in the church are excluded from divorce provisions under the civil law.

- For Hindus, the divorce is permitted only on the grounds of adultery by the wife.
- The law has inequalities in case of adopted and illegitimate children.

POLITICS OF GOA

The key political players in Goa state in Western India are the ruling Bharatiya Janata Party, Indian National Congress, Maharashtrawadi Gomantak Party and Goa Vikas Party.

National politics

There are only 2 Lok Sabha (lower house of the Indian Parliament) constituencies in Goa.

State politics

The Goa Legislative Assembly has 40 seats.

LIST OF GOVERNORS OF GOA

Mridula Sinha, the current Governor of Goa

The Governor of Goa is a nominal head and representative of the President of India in the state of Goa. The Governor is appointed by the President for a term of 5 years. Mridula Sinha became the Governor on 26 August 2014.

Powers and functions

The Governor has:

- Executive powers related to administration, appointments and removals,
- Legislative powers related to lawmaking and the state legislature, that is Vidhan Sabha or Vidhan Parishad, and
- Discretionary powers to be carried out according to the discretion of the Governor.

Ex officio powers

- The Governor is the Chancellor of the Goa University and exercises powers delegated under the Goa University Act, 1984 and the Statutes of the University.
- The Governor is the *ex officio* President of the Indian Red Cross Society, Goa Branch and has the powers to appoint the Chairman, Hon. Secretary, etc.
- The Governor is the President of the Goa State Environment Protection Council, which is an Advisory Body, set up by the Government of Goa. The Council consisting of Government Authorities and the NGOs engaged in environmental and the related areas meets once in six months and deliberates on various issues on the environment and ecology of the State.
- The Governor is the Chairman of the Special Fund for Rehabilitation and Reconstruction of Ex-Servicemen and Widows.

Portuguese Governors General

The first Portuguese Governor General was Francisco de Almeida in 1505 and the last Manuel Antonio Vassalo E Silva who left office in 1961. In total there have been 163 Governor Generals. For a complete list

Lieutenant Governors of Goa, Daman and Diu

Goa, along with Daman and Diu was a Union Territory in the Indian Union till 30 May 1987. As such it had a Lieutenant Governor till that time.

#	Name	Took Office	Left Office
1	Maj Gen K. P. Candeth (Military Governor)	19 December 1961	6 June 1962
2	T. Sivasankar	7 June 1962	1 September 1963
3	M. R. Sachdev	2 September 1963	8 December 1964
4	Hari Sharma	12 December 1964	23 February 1965
5	K. R. Damle	24 February 1965	17 April 1967
6	Nakul Sen	18 April 1967	15 November 1972
7	S. K. Banerji	16 November 1972	15 November 1977
8	P. S. Gill	16 November 1977	30 March 1981
9	Jagmohan	31 March 1981	29 August 1982
10	I H Latif	30 August 1982	23 February 1983
11	K. T. Satarawala	24 February 1983	3 July 1984
12	I H Latif	4 July 1984	23 September 1984
13	Gopal Singh	24 September 1984	29 May 1987

Governors after 1987

Goa became a full-fledged state of the Indian Union in 1987 and since then has had the following governors:

#	Name	Took Office	Left Office
1	Gopal Singh	30 May 1987	17 July 1989
2	Khurshed Alam Khan	18 July 1989	17 March 1991
3	Bhanu Prakash Singh	18 March 1991	3 April 1994
4	B. Rachaiah	4 April 1994	3 August 1994
5	Gopala Ramanujam	4 August 1994	15 June 1995
6	Romesh Bhandari	16 June 1995	18 July 1996
7	P.C. Alexander	19 July 1996	15 January 1998
8	T. R. Satish Chandran	16 January 1998	18 April 1998

9	J. F. R. Jacob	19 April 1998	26 November 1999
10	Mohammed Fazal	26 November 1999	25 October 2002
11	Kidar Nath Sahani	26 October 2002	2 July 2004
-	Mohammed Fazal (a.)	3 July 2004	16 July 2004
12	S. C. Jamir	17 July 2004	21 July 2008
13	Shivinder Singh Sidhu	22 July 2008	26 August 2011
14	Kateekal Sankaranarayanan	27 August 2011	3 May 2012
15	Bharat Vir Wanchoo	4 May 2012	4 July 2014
16	Margaret Alva	12 July 2014	5 August 2014
-	Om Prakash Kohli (a charge)		6 August 2014
25 August 2014			
17	Mridula Sinha	26 August 2014	Incumbent

4

Language and Literature

KONKANI LANGUAGE

Konkani is an Indo-Aryan language belonging to the Indo-European family of languages and is spoken by Konkani people along the western coast of India. It is one of the 22 scheduled languages mentioned in the 8th schedule of the Indian Constitution and the official language of the Indian state of Goa. The first Konkani inscription is dated 1187 A.D. It is a minority language in Karnataka, Maharashtra and Kerala, Dadra and Nagar Haveli, and Daman and Diu.

Konkani is a member of the southern Indo-Aryan language group. It retains elements of Proto-Dravidian structures and shows similarities with both western and eastern Indo-Aryan languages.

There are many fractured Konkani dialects, most of which are not mutually intelligible with one another.

Appellations

It is quite possible that Old Konkani was just referred to as *Prakrit* by its speakers. Among the inscriptions at the foot of the colossal statue of Bahubali at Shravanabelagola in

Karnataka are two lines reading thus: (i) Sri Chamundaraje Karaviyale and (ii) Sri Ganga raje sutthale karaviyale.

The first line was inscribed circa 981 AD and the second line in 116-17 AD.

The language of these lines is Konkani according to S.B. Kulkarni (former head of Department of Marathi, Nagpur University) and Jose Pereira (former professor, Fordham University, USA).

Considering these arguments, these inscriptions at Sravanabelegola may be considered the earliest Konkani inscriptions in Devanagari script. Reference to the name *Konkani* is not found in literature prior to the 13th century. The first reference of the name *Konkani* is in "Abhanga 263" of the 13th century Marathi saint poet, Namadeva (1270–1350). Konkani has been known by a variety of names: *Canarim, Concanim, Gomantaki, Bramana,* and *Goani.* It is called *Amchi Bhas* (our language) by native speakers (*Amchi Gele* in Dakshina Kannada), and *Govi* or *Goenchi Bhas* by others. Learned Marathi speakers tend to call it *Gomantaki.*

Konkani was commonly referred to as *Lingua Canarim* by the Portuguese and *Lingua Brahmana* by Catholic missionaries. The Portuguese later started referring to Konkani as *Lingua Concanim.*

The name *Canarim* or *Lingua Canarim*, which is how the 16th century European Jesuit, Thomas Stephens refers to it in the title of his famous work *Arte da lingoa Canarim* has always been intriguing. It is possible that the term is derived from the Persian word for coast, *kinara*; if so, it would mean "the language of the coast". The problem is that this term overlaps with *Kanarese* or Kannada.

All the European authors, however, recognised two forms of the language in Goa: the plebeian, called *Canarim*, and the more regular (used by the educated classes), called *Lingua Canarim Brámana* or simply *Brámana de Goa.* The latter was the preferred choice of the Europeans, and also of other castes, for writing, sermons, and religious purposes.

History

Etymology

There are different views as to the origin of the word Konkan and hence Konkani

- The word Konkan comes from the Kukkana tribe, who were the original inhabitants of the land where Konkani originated.
- According to some Hindu legends, Parashurama shot his arrow into the sea and commanded the Sea God to recede up to the point where his arrow landed.

Pre-history and early development

Konkani belongs to the Indo-Aryan language branch. It is inflexive, and less distant from Sanskrit as compared to other modern Indo-Aryan languages. Linguists describe Konkani as a fusion of variety of Prakrits. This could be attributed to the confluence of immigrants that the Konkan coast has witnessed over the years.Konkani developed with overall Sanskrit complexity and grammatical structure, which eventually developed into a lexical fund of its own. The second wave of Indo-Aryans is believed to have been accompanied by Dravidians from the Deccan plateau.

Goa and Konkan was ruled by the Konkan Mauryas and the Bhojas; as a result numerous migrations occurred from North, East and Western India. Immigrants spoke various vernaculars, which led to a mixture of features of Eastern and Western Prakrits. It was substantially influenced later by Magadhi Prakrit. The overtones of Pali (the liturgical language of the Buddhists) also played a very important role in the development of Konkani Apabhramsha grammar and vocabulary. A major number of linguistic innovations in Konkani are shared with Eastern Indo-Aryan languages like Bengali and Oriya, which have their roots in Magadhi.

Maharashtri was the official language of the Satavahana Empire that ruled Goa and Konkan in the early centuries of the Common Era. Under the patronage of the Satavahana Empire, Maharashtri became the most widespread Prakrit of its time. Studying early Maharashtri compilations, many linguists have called Konkani "the first-born daughter of Maharashtri". This old language that was prevalent contemporary to old Marathi is found to be distinct from its counterpart.

The Sauraseni impact on Konkani is not as prominent as that of Maharashtri. Very few Konkani words are found to follow the Sauraseni pattern. Konkani forms are rather more akin to Pali than the corresponding Sauraseni forms. The major Sauraseni influence on Konkani is the *ao* sound found at the end of many nouns in Sauraseni, which becomes *o* or *u* in Konkani. Examples include: *dando*, *suno*, *raakhano*, *dukh*, *rukhu*, *manisu* (from Prakrit), *dandao*, *sunnao*, *rakkhakao*, *dukkhao*, *vukkhao*, *vrukkhao*, and *mannisso*. Another example could be the sound of # at the beginning of words; it is still retained in many Konkani words of archaic Shauraseni origin, such as (nine). Archaic Konkani born out of Shauraseni vernacular Prakrit at the earlier stage of the evolution (and later Maharashtri Prakrit), was commonly spoken until 875 AD, and at its later phase ultimately developed into Apabhramsha, which could be called a predecessor of old Konkani.

The language

Although most of the stone inscriptions and copper plates found in Goa (and other parts of Konkan) from the 2nd century BC to the 10th century AD are in Prakrit-influenced Sanskrit (mostly written in early Brahmi and archaic Dravidian Brahmi), most of the places, grants, agricultural-related terms, and names of some people are in Konkani. This suggests that Konkani was spoken in Goa and Konkan.

Early Konkani

Another inscription in Nâgarî, of Shilahara King Aparaditya II of the year 1187 AD in Parel reportedly contains Konkani words, but this has not been reliably verified.Many stone and copper-plate inscriptions found in Goa and Konkan are written in Konkani. The grammar and the base of such texts is in Konkani, whereas very few verbs are in Marathi. Copper plates found in Ponda dating back to the early 13th century, and from Quepem in the early 14th century, have been written in Goykanadi. One such stone inscription or *shilalekh* (written Nâgarî) is found at the Nageshi temple in Goa (dating back to the year 1463 AD). It mentions that the (then) ruler of Goa, Devaraja Gominam, had gifted land to the Nagueshi Maharudra temple when Nanjanna Gosavi was the religious head or *Pratihasta* of the state. It mentions words like, *kullgga, kulaagra, naralel, tambavem*, and *tilel.*

Medieval Konkani

This era was marked by the invasion of Goa and subsequent exodus to Marhatta territory, Canara (today's coastal Karnataka), and Cochin.

- Exodus (between 1312–1327) when General Malik Kafur of the Delhi Sultans, Alauddin Khalji, and Muhammed bin Tughlaq destroyed Govepuri and the Kadambas
- Exodus subsequent to 1470 when the Bahamani kingdom captured Goa, and subsequent capture in 1492 by Sultan Yusuf Adil Shah of Bijapur
- Exodus due to the Christianization of Goa by Portuguese subsequent to 1500
- Hindu, Muslim, and Neo-Catholic Christian exodus during the Goa Inquisition, which was established in 1560 and abolished in 1812.

These events caused the Konkani language to evolve into multiple dialects. The exodus to coastal Karnataka and Kerala required Konkani speakers in these regions to learn the local languages. This caused penetration of local words into the dialects of Konkani spoken by these speakers. Examples include *dâr* (door) giving way to the word *bâgil.* Also, the phoneme "a" in the Salcette dialect was replaced by the phoneme "o".

Other Konkani communities came into being with their own

dialects of Konkani. The Konkani Muslim communities of Ratnagiri and Bhatkal came about due to a mixture of intermarriages of Arab seafarers and locals as well as conversions of Hindus to Islam. Another migrant community that picked up Konkani are the Siddis, who are descended from Bantu peoples from South East Africa that were brought to the Indian subcontinent as slaves by Portuguese merchants.

Contemporary Konkani

Contemporary Konkani is written in Devanagari, Kannada, Malayalam, Persian, and Roman scripts. It is written by speakers in their native dialects. However, the Goan Antruz dialect in the Devanagari script has been promulgated as Standard Konkani.

Geographical distribution

The Konkani language is spoken widely in the western coastal region of India known as Konkan. This consists of the Konkan division of Maharashtra, the state of Goa, and the Uttara Kannada (formerly North Canara), Udupi, and Dakshina Kannada(formerly South Canara) districts of Karnataka, together with many districts in Kerala (such as Kasargod, Kochi, Alappuzha, Trivandrum, and Kottayam). Each region has a different dialect, pronunciation style, vocabulary, tone and sometimes, significant differences in grammar. According to the 2001 estimates of the Census Department of India, there were 2,489,016 Konkani speakers in India. The Census Department of India, 2011 figures put the number of Konkani speakers in India as 2,256,502 making up 0.19% of India's population. Out of these, 788,294 were in Karnataka, 964,305 in Goa,399,255 in Maharashtra, and 69,449 in Kerala. It ranks 19th on the List of Scheduled Languages by strength. The number of Konkani speakers in India fell by 9.34% in the decade 2001-2011. It is the only scheduled language apart from Urdu to have a negative growth rate in the decade. A very large number of Konkanis live outside India, either as expatriates or citizens of other countries (NRIs). Determining their numbers is difficult.

A significant number of Konkani speakers are found in Kenya, Uganda, Pakistan, the Persian Gulf, and Portugal. During Portuguese rule many Goans had migrated to these countries. Many families still continue to speak different dialects that their ancestors spoke, which are now highly influenced by the native languages.

Konkani revival

Konkani was in a sorry state, due to the use of Portuguese as the official and social language among the Christians, the predominance of Marathi over Konkani among Hindus, and the Konkani Christian-Hindu divide. Seeing this, Vaman Raghunath Varde Valaulikar set about on a mission to unite all Konkanis, Hindus as well as Christians, regardless of caste or religion. He saw this movement not just as a nationalistic movement against Portuguese rule, but also against the pre-eminence of Marathi over Konkani. Almost single-handedly he crusaded, writing a number of works in Konkani. He is regarded as the pioneer of modern Konkani literature and affectionately remembered as Shenoi Goembab. His death anniversary, 9 April, is celebrated as World Konkani Day (Vishwa Konkani Dis).

Madhav Manjunath Shanbhag, an advocate by profession from Karwar, who with a few like-minded companions travelled throughout all the Konkani speaking areas, sought to unite the fragmented Konkani community under the banner of "one language, one script, one literature". He succeeded in organising the first All India Konkani Parishad in Karwar in 1939. Successive Adhiveshans of All India Konkani Parishad were held at various places in subsequent years. 27 annual Adhiveshans of All India Konkani Parishad have been held so far.

Pandu Putti Kolambkar an eminent social worker of Kodibag, Karwar strove for the upliftment of Konkani in Karwar (North Kanara) and Konkan.

Post-independence period

Following India's independence and its subsequent annexation of Goa in 1961, Goa was absorbed into the Indian Union as a Union Territory, directly under central administration.

However, with the reorganisation of states along linguistic lines, and growing calls from Maharashtra, as well as Marathis in Goa for the merger of Goa into Maharashtra, an intense debate was started in Goa. The main issues discussed were the status of Konkani as an independent language and Goa's future as a part of Maharashtra or as an independent state. A plebiscite retained Goa as an independent state in 1967. However, English, Hindi, and Marathi continued to be the preferred languages for official communication, while Konkani was sidelined.

Recognition as an independent language

With the continued insistence of some Marathis that Konkani was a dialect of Marathi and not an independent language, the matter was finally placed before the Sahitya Akademi. Suniti Kumar Chatterji, the president of the Akademi appointed a committee of linguistic experts to settle the dispute. On 26 February 1975, the committee came to the conclusion that Konkani was indeed an independent and literary language, classified as an Indo-European language, which in its present state was heavily influenced by the Portuguese language.

Official language status

All this did not change anything in Goa. Finally fed up with the delay, Konkani enthusiasts launched an agitation in 1986, demanding official status for Konkani. The agitation turned violent in various places, resulting in the death of six agitators from the Catholic community: Floriano Vaz from Gogal Margao, Aldrin Fernandes, Mathew Faria, C. J. Dias, John Fernandes, and Joaquim Pereira, all from Agaçaim. Finally, on 4 February 1987, the Goa Legislative Assembly passed the Official Language Bill, making Konkani the official language of Goa.

Konkani was included in the Eighth Schedule to the Constitution of India as per the Seventy-First Amendment on 20 August 1992, adding it to the list of national languages.

Phonology

The Konkani language has 16 basic vowels (excluding an equal number of long vowels), 36 consonants, 5 semi-vowels, 3 sibilants, 1 aspirate, and many diphthongs. Like the other Indo-Aryan languages, it has both long and short vowels and syllables with long vowels may appear to be stressed. Different types of nasal vowels are a special feature of the Konkani language.

- The palatal and alveolar stops are affricates. The palatal glides are truly palatal but otherwise the consonants in the palatal column are alveopalatal.
- The voiced/voiceless contrasts are found only in the stops and affricates. The fricatives are all voiceless and the sonorants are all voiced.
- The initial vowel-syllable is shortened after the aspirates and fricatives. Many speakers substitute unaspirated consonants for aspirates.
- Aspirates in a non-initial position are rare and only occur in careful speech. Palatalisation/non-palatisation is found in all obstruents, except for palatal and alveolars. Where a palatalised alveolar is expected, a palatal is found instead. In the case of sonorants, only unaspirated consonants show this contrast, and among the glides only labeo-velar glides exhibit this. Vowels show a contrast between oral and nasal ones

Vowels

One of the most distinguishing features of Konkani phonology is the use of /u□/, the close-mid central vowel, instead of the schwa as used in Hindi-Urdu and Marathi.

Whereas many Indian languages use only one of the three front vowels, represented by the Devanagari grapheme, Konkani uses three: /e/, /[□/ and /æ/. Nasalizations exist for all vowels except for /□/.

MARATHI LANGUAGE

Marathi is an Indo-Aryan language spoken predominantly by around 83 million Marathi people of Maharashtra, India. It is the official language and co-official language in the Maharashtra and Goa states of Western India, respectively, and is one of the 22 scheduled languages of India. There were 83 million speakers in 2011; Marathi ranks 19th in the list of most spoken languages in the world. Marathi has the third largest number of native speakers in India, after Hindi and Bengali. Marathi has some of the oldest literature of all modern Indian languages, dating from about 900 AD. The major dialects of Marathi are Standard Marathi and the Varhadi dialect. Koli, Malvani Konkani has been heavily influenced by Marathi varieties.

Marathi distinguishes inclusive and exclusive forms of 'we' and possesses a three-way gender system that features the neuter in addition to the masculine and the feminine. In its phonology it contrasts apico-alveolar with alveopalatalaffricates and, in common with Gujarati, alveolar with retroflex laterals.

Geographic distribution

Marathi is primarily spoken in Maharashtra (India) and parts of neighbouring states of Gujarat, Madhya Pradesh, Goa,Karnataka (Particularly the bordering districts of Belgaum, Bidar, Gulbarga and Uttara Kannada), union-territories of Daman and Diu and Dadra and Nagar Haveli. The former Maratha ruled cities of Baroda, Indore, Gwalior, Jabalpur and Tanjore have had sizable Marathi speaking populations for centuries. Marathi is also spoken by Maharashtrian emigrants to other parts of India and overseas.

There were 83 million native Marathi speakers in India, according to the 2011 census, making it the third most spoken native language after Hindi and Bengali. Native Marathi speakers form 6.86 % of India's population. Native speakers of Marathi formed 68.93% of the population in Maharashtra, 10.89% in Goa, 7.01% in Dadra and Nagar Haveli, 4.53% in Daman and Diu, 3.38% in Karnataka, 1.7% in Madhya Pradesh and 1.52% in Gujarat.

Status

Marathi is the official language of Maharashtra and co-official language in the union territories of Daman and Diu and Dadra and Nagar Haveli. In Goa, Konkani is the sole official language; however, Marathi may also be used for some official purposes in some case. Marathi is included among the languages which stand a part of the Eighth Schedule of the Constitution of India, thus granting it the status of a "scheduled language". The Government of Maharashtra has submitted an application to the Ministry of Culture to grant *classical language* status to Marathi.

The contemporary grammatical rules described by Maharashtra Sahitya Parishad and endorsed by the Government of Maharashtraare supposed to take precedence in standard written Marathi. Traditions of Marathi Linguistics and the above-mentioned rules give special status to tatsamas, words adapted from Sanskrit. This special status expects the rules for tatsamas to be followed as in Sanskrit. This practice provides Marathi with a large treasure of Sanskrit words to cope with demands of new technical words whenever needed.

In addition to all universities in Maharashtra, Maharaja Sayajirao University of Baroda in Vadodara, Osmania University in Hyderabad, Karnataka University in Dharwad, Gulbarga University in Kalaburagi, Devi Ahilya University in Indore and Goa University in Goa have special departments for higher studies in Marathi linguistics. Jawaharlal Nehru University (New Delhi) has announced plans to establish a special department for Marathi.

Marathi Day is celebrated on 27 February, the birthday of the poet Kusumagraj (Vishnu Vaman Shirwadkar).

History

The earliest example of Maharashtri as a separate language dates to approximately 3rd century BCE: a stone inscription found in a cave at Naneghat, Junnar in Pune district had been written in Maharashtri using Brahmi script. A committee appointed by the Maharashtra State Government to get the Classical status for Marathi has claimed that Marathi existed at least 2300 years ago alongside Sanskrit as a sister language. Marathi, a derivative of Maharashtri, is probably first attested in a 739 CE copper-plate inscription found in Satara. Several inscriptions dated to the second half of the 11th century feature Marathi, which is usually appended to Sanskrit or Kannada in these inscriptions. The earliest Marathi-only inscriptions are the ones issued during the Shilahara rule, including a c. 1012 CE stone inscription from Akshi taluka of Raigad district, and a 1060 or 1086 CE copper-plate inscription from Dive that records a land grant (*agrahara*) to a Brahmin. A 2-line 1118 CE Marathi inscription at Shravanabelagola records a grant by the Hoysalas. These inscriptions suggest that Marathi was a standard written language by the 12th century. However, there is no record of any actual literature produced in Marathi until the late 13th century.

Yadava period

After 1187 CE, the use of Marathi grew substantially in the inscriptions of the Seuna (Yadava) kings, who earlier used Kannada and Sanskrit in their inscriptions.Marathi became the dominant language of epigraphy during the last half century of the dynasty's rule (14th century), and may have been a result of the Yadava attempts to connect with their Marathi-speaking subjects and to distinguish themselves from the Kannada-speaking Hoysalas.

Further growth and usage of the language was because of two religious sects – the Mahanubhava and Varkari *panthan*s – who adopted Marathi as the medium for preaching their doctrines of devotion. Marathi had attained a venerable place in court life by the time of the Seuna kings. During the reign of the last three Seuna kings, a great deal of literature in verse and prose, on astrology, medicine, Puranas, Vedanta, kings and courtiers were created. *Nalopakhyan*, *Rukmini swayamvar* and Shripati's *Jyotishratnamala* (1039) are a few examples.

The oldest book in prose form in Marathi, *Vivçkasindhu*, was written by Mukundaraja, a Nath yogi and arch-poet of Marathi. Mukundaraja bases his exposition of the basic tenets of the Hindu philosophy and the yoga marga on the utterances or teachings of Shankaracharya. Mukundaraja's other work, *Paramamrta,*is considered the first systematic attempt to explain the Vedanta in the Marathi language

Medieval and Deccan Sultanate period

The 13th-century varkari saint Dnyaneshwar(1275–1296) wrote a treatise in Marathi on Bhagawat Gita popularly called *Dnyaneshwari* and *Amritanubhava*. His contemporary, Namdev composed verses or abhang in Marathi as well as Hindi.

Mukund Raj was a poet who lived in the 13th century and is said to be the first poet who composed in Marathi. He is known for the *Viveka-Siddhi* and *Parammrita*which are metaphysical, pantheistic works connected with orthodox Vedantism.

The 16th century saint-poet Eknath (1528–1599) is well known for composing the Eknâthî Bhâgavat, a commentary on Bhagavat Purana and the devotional songs called Bharud. Mukteshwar translated the *Mahabharata* into Marathi; Tukaram (1608–49) transformed Marathi into a rich literary language. His poetry contained his inspirations. Tukaram wrote over 3000 abhangs or devotional songs.

Maratha Empire

Marathi gained prominence with the rise of the Maratha Empire beginning with the reign of Chhatrapati Shivaji Maharaj (ruled 1674–1680). Under Shivaji, the language used in administrative documents became less persianised. Whereas in

1630, 80% of the vocabulary was Persian, it dropped to 37% by 1677 Samarth Ramdaswas a contemporary of Shivaji. He advocated the unity of Marathas to propagate Maharashtra dharma. Unlike varkari saints, his writing has a strong militant expression to it. Subsequent Maratha rulers extended the empire northwards to Attock, eastwards to Odisha, and southwards to Thanjavur in Tamil Nadu. These excursions by the Marathas helped to spread Marathi over broader geographical regions. This period also saw the use of Marathi in transactions involving land and other business. Documents from this period, therefore, give a better picture of the life of common people. There are a lot of Bakharis written in Marathi and Modi script from this period. But by the late 18th century, the Maratha Empire's influence over a large part of the country was on the decline.

In the 18th century during Peshwa rule, some well-known works such as Yatharthadeepika by Vaman Pandit, Naladamayanti Swayamvara by Raghunath Pandit, Pandava Pratap, Harivijay, Ramvijay by Shridhar Pandit and Mahabharata by Moropant were produced. Krishnadayarnava and Sridhar were poets during the Peshwaperiod. New literary forms were successfully experimented with during the period and classical styles were revived, especially the Mahakavya and Prabandha forms. The most important hagiographies of Varkari Bhakti saints was written by Mahipati in the 18th Century. Other well known literary scholars of the 17th century were Mukteshwar and Shridhar. Mukteshwar was the grandson of Eknath and is the most distinguished poet in the *Ovi* meter. He is most known for translating the Mahabharata and the Ramayana in Marathi but only a part of the Mahabharata translation is available and the entire Ramayana translation is lost. Shridhar Kulkarni came from the Pandharpur area and his works are said to have superseded the Sanskrit epics to a certain extent. This period also saw the development of Powada (ballads sung in honor of warriors), and Lavani (romantic songs presented with dance and instruments like tabla). Major poet composers of Powada and Lavani songs of the 17th and the 18th century were Anant Phandi, Ram Joshi and Honaji Bala.

British colonial period

The British colonial period starting in early 1800s saw standardisation of Marathi grammar through the efforts of the Christian missionary William Carey. Carey's dictionary had fewer entries and Marathi words were in Devanagari. Translations of the Bible were first books to be printed in Marathi.These translations by William Carey, the American Marathi mission and the Scottish missionaries led to the development of a peculiar pidginized Marathi called the "Missionary Marathi in early 1800s The most comprehensive Marathi-English dictionary was compiled by Captain James Thomas Molesworth and Major Thomas Candy in 1831. The book is still in print nearly two centuries after its publication. The colonial authorities also worked on standardizing Marathi under the leadership of James Thomas Molesworth and Candy. They used Brahmins of Pune for this task and adopted the Sanskrit dominated dialect spoken by the elite in the city as the standard dialect for Marathi.

The first Marathi translation of the New Testament was published in 1811 by the Serampore press of William Carey. The first Marathi newspaper called Durpan was started by Balshastri Jambhekar in 1832. Newspapers provided a platform for sharing literary views, and many books on social reforms were written. First Marathi periodical *Dirghadarshan* was started in 1840. The Marathi language flourished, as Marathi drama gained popularity. Musicals known as *Sangeet Natak* also evolved. Keshavasut, the father of modern Marathi poetry published his first poem in 1885. The late-19th century in Maharashtra saw the rise of essayistVishnushastri Chiplunkar with his periodical, Nibandhmala that had essays that criticized social reformers like Phule and Gopal Hari Deshmukh. Phule and Deshmukh also started their own periodicals, *Deenbandhu* and *Prabhakar*, that criticised the prevailing Hindu culture of the day. The 19th century and early 20th century saw several books published on Marathi Grammar. Notable grammarians of this period were Tarkhadkar, A.K.Kher, Moro Keshav Damle, and R.Joshi

The first half of the 20th century was marked by new enthusiasm in literary pursuits, and socio-political activism helped achieve major milestones in Marathi literature, drama, music and film. Modern Marathi prose flourished through various new literary forms like the essay, the biographies, the novels, prose, drama etc. N.C.Kelkar's biographical writings, novels of Hari Narayan Apte, Narayan Sitaram Phadke and V. S. Khandekar, Vinayak Damodar Savarkar's nationalist literature and plays of Mama Varerkar and Kirloskar are particularly worth noting.

Marathi since Indian independence

After Indian independence, Marathi was accorded the status of a scheduled language on the national level.In 1956, the then Bombay state was reorganized which brought most Marathi and Gujarati speaking areas under one state.Further re-organization of the Bombay state on May 1, 1960 created the Marathi speaking Maharashtra and Gujarati speaking Gujarat state respectively.With state and cultural protection, Marathi made great strides by the 1990s. A literary event called *Akhil Bharatiya Marathi Sahitya Sammelan* (All-India Marathi Literature Meet) is held every year. In addition, the *Akhil Bharatiya Marathi Natya Sammelan* (All-India Marathi Theatre Convention) is also held annually. Both events are very popular among Marathi speakers.

The Marathi spoken by Chitpavan in Pune is the standard form of language used all over Maharashtra today. This form has many words derived from Sansrkrit and retains the Sanskrit pronunciation of many, misconstrued by non-standard speakers as "nasalised pronunciation".

Notable works in Marathi in the latter half of 20th century include Khandekar's Yayati, which won him the Jnanpith Award. Also Vijay Tendulkar's plays in Marathi have earned him a reputation beyond Maharashtra. P.L.Deshpande(PuLa), Vishnu Vaman Shirwadkar, P.K.Atre & Prabodhankar Thackeray, were also known for their writings in Marathi in the field of drama, comedy and social commentary

In 1958 the term "Dalit literature" was used for the first time, when the first conference of *Maharashtra Dalit Sahitya Sangha* (Maharashtra Dalit Literature Society) was held at Mumbai, a movement inspired by 19th century social reformer, Jyotiba Phule and eminent dalit leader, Dr. Bhimrao Ambedkar. Baburao Bagul (1930–2008) was a pioneer of Dalit writings in Marathi. His first collection of stories, *Jevha Mi Jat Chorali*(When I Concealed My Caste), published in 1963, created a stir in Marathi literature with its passionate depiction of a cruel society and thus brought in new momentum to Dalit literature in Marathi. Gradually with other writers like, Namdeo Dhasal (who founded Dalit Panther), these Dalit writings paved way for the strengthening of Dalit movement. Notable Dalit authors writing in Marathi include Arun Kamble, Shantabai Kamble, Raja Dhale, Namdev Dhasal, Daya Pawar, Annabhau Sathe, Laxman Mane, Laxman Gaikwad, Sharankumar Limbale, Bhau Panchbhai, Kishor Shantabai Kale, Narendra jadhav, and Urmila Pawar.

In recent decades there has been a trend among Marathi speaking parents of all social classes in major urban areas of sending their children to English medium schools. There is some concern, though without foundation, that this may lead to the marginalization of the language.

Dialects

Indic scholars distinguish 42 dialects of spoken Marathi. Dialects bordering other major language areas have many properties in common with those languages, further differentiating them from standard spoken Marathi. The bulk of the variation within these dialects is primarily lexical and phonological (e.g. accent placement and pronunciation). Although the number of dialects is considerable, the degree of intelligibility within these dialects is relatively high.

Zadi Boli

Zadi Boli or Zhadiboli is spoken in Zadipranta (a forest rich region) of far eastern Maharashtra or eastern Vidarbha or western-central Gondwana comprising Gondia, Bhandara,

Chandrapur, Gadchiroli and some parts of Nagpur of Maharashtra.

Zadi Boli Sahitya Mandal and many literary figures are working for the conservation of this important and distinct dialect of Marathi.

Southern Indian Marathi

Thanjavur Marathi, Namadeva Shimpi Marathi, Arey Marathi and Bhavsar Marathi are some of the dialects of Marathi spoken by many descendants of Maharashtrians who migrated to the Southern India.

These dialects retain the 17th-century basic form of Marathi and have been considerably influenced by the Dravidian languages after the migration. These dialects have speakers in various parts of Tamil Nadu, Andhra Pradesh and Karnataka.

Varhadi

Varhadi (Varhâdi) or *Vaidarbhi* is spoken in the Western Vidarbha region of Maharashtra. In Marathi, the retroflex lateral approximant *7*□ [m□] is common, while in the Varhadii dialect, it corresponds to the palatal , making this dialect quite distinct. Such phonetic shifts are common in spoken Marathi and, as such, the spoken dialects vary from one region of Maharashtra to another.

Others

- Thanjavur Marathi, spoken in Tanjore, Tamil Nadu
- Judæo-Marathi, spoken by the Bene Israel Jews

Other Languages and dialects spoken in Maharashtra include Maharashtrian Konkani, Koli, Malvani, Agri, Andh, Warli, Dangi, Khandeshi, Ahirani, Kokna, Vadvali, Samavedi, Marathwadi and Deshi.

GOAN LITERATURE

Goan literature is the literature pertaining to the state of Goa in India.

Goan Literature

Goa has a population of around 1.4 million and an area of 3,700 sq. kilometres (1,430 sq. miles). For a small region, it has a significant amount of publication activity, possibly in part because its people write in a number of languages—perhaps as many as 13—and also because of the large expatriate and diaspora population of Goans settled across the globe.

Among its most noted writers are Laxmanrao Sardessai (1904-1986) and R. V. Pandit (1917-1990), both of whom wrote poetry and prose in Marathi, Konkani, and Portuguese; Shenoi Goembab (1877–1946), whose Konkani writing helped to establish Konkani as a modern literary language; Ravindra Kelekar (1925-2010), who wrote some of the twentieth century's foremost Konkani literature; and Pundalik Naik (1952-), whose 1977 novel *Acchev* was the first Konkani novel to be translated into English.

History

Goa was the first place in Asia to have a printing press, which was brought by the Jesuits in 1556. Nearly all of Goan literature before that time is known to have been destroyed by the Portuguese during the imposition of Inquisition. Goa's Portuguese colonial rulers can hardly be credited with meticulous record-keeping of Goan literature. Thus, Goa has had a long love affair with the written and printed word, although growth has been slow, and punctuated by problems like linguistic breaks and censorship.

Peter Nazareth points out that Goans have written in thirteen languages, of which the chief are Konkani, Marathi, English and Portuguese. Nazareth describes Goans as 'cultural brokers':

Goans mediate between cultures, Goans live between different cultures, Goans are travellers from one part of the world to another. This, in my opinion, happened when East and West met in Goans under pressure with the Portuguese conquest. Since that time, our usefulness to the world, wherever we are, is that we can understand different cultures and help people from different cultures understand one another. The disadvantage is that if we don't work on it, we may end up not knowing who we are.

Literary writing in Goa began to take shape under Portuguese rule and influence, associated with Portugal's mid-nineteenth-century Regeneration, which saw the reintroduction of the press to Goa, along with expanded Portuguese education. A spate of Portuguese-language publications, 'such as *A Biblioteca de Goa* (1839), *O Enciclopédico* (1841-1842), *O Compilador* (1843-1847), *O Gabinete Literário das Fontainhas* (1846-1848), *A revista Ilustrativa* (1857-1866) and *O Arquivo Portugués Oriental* (1857-1866)', along with Júlio Gonçalves's *Ilustraçao Goana* (1864-1866), while often short-lived, provided new fora not only for the circulation of European literature (whether originally in Portuguese or in translation), but provided growing opportunities for Goans to publish literary and scholarly writing.

The first novel published by a Goan was *Os Brahamanes* (*The Brahmans*) by Francisco Luis Gomes, published in 1866.

Later in the nineteenth century, vernacular writing began to emerge in strength, for example in Konkani, the widely spoken local vernacular. The Goan writer Shenoi Goembab (1877–1946) was foundational to developing modern Konkani literature. An official language of the region since 1987, Konkani is now studied in schools. Konkani literature emerged alongside the rapid growth of Marathi literature, in which the Goan R. V. Pandit was a notable exponent. S. M. Tadkodkar, who was conferred Ph.D. degree by Goa University for his exhaustive research work on Anant Kaakaba Priolkar, contends that while the Kannadd language of Karnataka province was dominating the Goan culture, Marathi language and culture was embraced by Goans. Now, Marathi has embraced the Goans and would not leave them, willingly. Maximum literature is published in Marathi. There are 8 Marathi dailies published from Goa. Prominent among them are *Dianik Gomantak, Tarun Bharat, Lokamat, Navaprabha, Pudhari, Goadoot, Sanatan Prabhat.* The Marathi daily *Lokmat* has the highest circulation (50000+) among all dailies.

In the late nineteenth century, extensive contacts with and migration to British-ruled India also encouraged English-language Goan writing, with early exponents including Joseph Furtado. Edward D'Lima, who has done his PhD on the Goan writer Armando Menezes, argues that Goan writing in English goes back to the late nineteenth century, when Goans were migrating out of this Portuguese-controlled colony in favour of jobs in the growing English-speaking British-ruled colonial world.

English is probably the most influential literary language in Goa: 'a surge of creativity has erupted in Goan literature in English since 2000 in fiction and nonfiction, drama and poetry'.

5

Geography and Flora & Fauna

GEOGRAPHY AND CLIMATE

Geography

Goa encompasses an area of 3,702 km (1,429 sq mi). It lies between the latitudes 14°532543 N and 15°402003 N and longitudes 73°402333 E and 74°202133 E.

Goa is a part of the coastal country known as the Konkan, which is an escarpment rising up to the Western Ghats range of mountains, which separate it from the Deccan Plateau. The highest point is the Sonsogor, with an altitude of 1,167 metres (3,829 ft). Goa has a coastline of 101 km (63 mi).

Goa's seven major rivers are the Zuari, Mandovi, Terekhol, Chapora, Galgibag, Kumbarjua canal, Talpona and the Sal. The Zuari and the Mandovi are the most important rivers, interspaced by the Kumbarjua canal, forming a major estuarine complex. These rivers are fed by the Southwest monsoon rain and their basin covers 69% of the state's geographical area. These rivers are some of the busiest in India. Goa has more than 40 estuarine, eight marine, and about 90 riverine islands. The total navigable length of Goa's rivers is 253 km (157 mi).

Goa has more than 300 ancient water-tanks built during the rule of the Kadamba dynasty and over 100 medicinal springs.

Goa coastline at Dona Paula

The Mormugao harbour on the mouth of the River Zuari is one of the best natural harbours in South Asia.

Most of Goa's soil cover is made up of laterites rich in ferric-aluminium oxides and reddish in colour. Further inland and along the riverbanks, the soil is mostly alluvial and loamy. The soil is rich in minerals and humus, thus conducive to agriculture. Some of the oldest rocks in the Indian subcontinent are found in Goa between Molem and Anmod on Goa's border with Karnataka. The rocks are classified as Trondjemeitic Gneissestimated to be 3,600 million years old, dated by rubidium isotope dating. A specimen of the rock is exhibited at Goa University.

Climate

Goa features a tropical monsoon climate under the Köppen climate classification. Goa, being in the tropical zone and near the Arabian Sea, has a hot and humid climate for most of the year. The month of May is usually the hottest, seeing daytime temperatures of over 35 °C (95 °F) coupled with high humidity. The state's three seasons are: Southwest monsoon period (June – September), post-monsoon period (October – January) and fair weather period (February – May). Over 90% of the average annual rainfall (120 inches) is received during the monsoon season.

Dudhsagar Falls on the Goa-Karnataka border

Subdivisions

The state is divided into two districts: North Goa and South Goa. Each district is administered by a district collector, appointed by the Indian government.

Panaji is the headquarters of North Goa district and is also the capital of Goa.

North Goa is further divided into three subdivisions – Panaji, Mapusa, and Bicholim; and five taluks – Ilhas de Goa (Tiswadi), Bardez (Mapusa), Pernem, Bicholim, and Sattari (Valpoi),

Margão is the headquarters of South Goa district.

South Goa is further divided into five subdivisions – Ponda, Mormugao (Vasco da Gama), Margao, Quepem, and Dharbandora; and seven *taluks* – Ponda, Mormugao, Salcete (Margao), Quepem, and Canacona (Chaudi), Sanguem, and Dharbandora. (Ponda Taluka shifted from North Goa to South Goa in January 2015).

Goa's major cities include Panaji, Margao, Vasco da Gama, Mapusa, Ponda and Valpoi.

Panaji has the only Municipal Corporation in Goa.

There are thirteen Municipal Councils: Margao, Mormugao (including Vasco da Gama), Pernem, Mapusa, Bicholim, Sanquelim, Valpoi, Ponda, Cuncolim, Quepem, Curchorem, Sanguem, and Canacona. Goa has a total number of 334 villages.

FLORA AND FAUNA OF GOA

Coconut palm trees are a ubiquitous symbol of the State

Equatorial forest cover in Goa stands at 1,424 km (549.81 sq mi), most of which is owned by the government. Government owned forest is estimated at 1,224.38 km (472.74 sq mi) whilst private is given as 200 km (77.22 sq mi). Most of the forests in the state are located in the interior eastern regions of the state. The Western Ghats, which form most of eastern Goa, have been internationally recognised as one of the biodiversity hotspots of the world. In the February 1999 issue of *National Geographic Magazine*, Goa was compared with the Amazon and the Congo basins for its rich tropical biodiversity. Goa's wildlife sanctuaries boast of more than 1512 documented species of plants, over 275 species of birds, over 48 kinds of animals and over 60 genera of reptiles.

Goa is also known for its coconut cultivation. The coconut tree has been reclassified by the government as a palm (like a grass), enabling farmers and real estate developers to clear land with fewer restrictions.

Rice is the main food crop, and pulses (legume), *Ragi* (Finger Millet) and other food crops are also grown. Main cash crops are coconut, cashewnut, arecanut, sugarcane and fruits like pineapple, mango and banana. Goa's state animal is the Gaur, the state bird is the Ruby Throated Yellow Bulbul, which is a variation of Black-crested Bulbul, and the state tree is the Matti(Asna).

Rice paddies are common in rural Goa

The important forests products are bamboo canes, Maratha barks, chillar barks and the bhirand. Coconut trees are ubiquitous and are present in almost all areas of Goa barring the elevated regions. A large number of deciduous trees, such as teak, Sal tree, cashew and mango trees are present. Fruits include jackfruit, mango, pineapple and "black-berry" ("podkoam" in Konkani language). Goa's forests are rich with medicinal plants.

Foxes, wild boar and migratory birds are found in the jungles of Goa. The avifauna (bird species) includes kingfisher, *myna* and parrot.

Numerous types of fish are also caught off the coast of Goa and in its rivers. Crab, lobster, shrimp, jellyfish, oysters and catfish are the basis of the marine fishery. Goa also has a high snake population.

Goa has many famous "National Parks", including the renowned Salim Ali Bird Sanctuary on the island of Chorão. Other wildlife sanctuaries include the Bondla Wildlife Sanctuary, Molem Wildlife Sanctuary, Cotigao Wildlife Sanctuary, Madei Wildlife Sanctuary, Netravali Wildlife Sanctuary, and Mahaveer Wildlife Sanctuary.

Goa has more than 33% of its geographic area under government forests (1224.38 km^2) of which about 62% has been brought under Protected Areas (PA) of Wildlife Sanctuaries and National Park. Since there is a substantial area under private forests and a large tract under cashew, mango, coconut, etc. plantations, the total forest and tree cover constitutes 56.6% of the geographic area.

SALIM ALI BIRD SANCTUARY

Salim Ali Bird Sanctuary is an estuarine mangrove habitat, which is declared as the bird sanctuary, and located on western tip of the Island of Chorão along the Mandovi River, Goa, in India. The sanctuary is named after Salim Ali, the eminent Indian ornithologist.

The sanctuary and island are accessed by a ferry service running between Ribander and Chorão. The sanctuary has a paved walk that runs between mangroves of *Rhizophora mucronata*, *Avicennia officinalis* and other species.

Description

Paved walkway inside the sanctuary

The size of the sanctuary is 178 ha (440 acres). The area is covered by low mangrove forest.

Flora and fauna

Salim Ali Bird sanctuary is one of the best-known bird sanctuaries in India

Several species of birds have been recorded and the common species include the striated heron and western reef heron. Other species that have been recorded include the little bittern, black bittern, red knot, jack snipe and pied avocet (on transient sandbanks). The sanctuary is also host to mudskippers, fiddler crabs and other mangrove habitat specialists. A species of crustacean *Teleotanais indianis* was described based on specimens obtained in the sanctuary.

DISTRICTS

North Goa

North Goa is one of the two districts that make up the state of Goa, India. The district has an area of 1736 km^2, and is bounded by Ratnagiri and Kolhapur districts of Maharashtra state to the north and east respectively, by South Goa District to the south, and by the Arabian Sea to the west.

The administrative headquarters of the district is Panaji, which is also the capital of the state of Goa. The district is divided into four subdivisions, Panaji, Mapusa, Bicholim, and Ponda, and six taluks, Bardez, Bicholim, Pernem, Ponda, Sattari and Tiswadi.

Goa was a Portuguese colony from 1510 until December 1961, when it was annexed by India. Goa and two other former Portuguese enclaves became the union territory of Goa, Daman and Diu, and Goa was organized into a single district in 1965. On 30 May 1987, Goa attained statehood (while Daman and Diu remained a union territory), and Goa was reorganized into two districts, North Goa and South Goa.

South Goa

South Goa is one of the two districts that comprise the state of Goa, India. The district has an area of 1,966 km^2 and a population of 586,591 (2001 census). It is bounded by North Goa District to the north, Utara Kannada District of Karnataka state to the east and south, and by the Arabian Sea to the west.

The administrative headquarters of the district is Madgaon. The district is divided into three subdivisions, Margao, Mormugao, and Quepem, and five taluks, Salcete, Mormugao, Quepem, Sanguem, and Canacona.

The Portuguese established a colony in Goa in 1510, and expanded the colony to its present boundaries during the 17th and 18th centuries. Goa was annexed by India on December 19, 1961. Goa and two other former Portuguese enclaves became the union territory of Goa, Daman and Diu, and Goa was organized into a single district in 1965. On 30 May 1987 Goa attained statehood (while Daman and Diu became a separate union territory), and Goa was reorganized into two districts, North Goa and South Goa.

CITIES AND TOWNS

Aldona

Aldona is a village in Bardez, and a census town in the North Goa district in the state of Goa, India.

Its church is dedicated to Sao Tome. The parish chapels include the chapel at Carona (Sta. Rita de Cascia), Corjuem (Mae de Deus) and the one at Quitula.

It has several *vadde*, including Quitula, Udoim, Coimavaddo, Carona, Santerxette, Naikavaddo, Panarim and Ranoi.

Aldona is connected to Corjuem by a state of the art cable-stayed bridge held by six cables from either direction.

The current Archbishop of Goa and Daman, India, Filipe Neri Antonio Sebastiao do Rosario Ferrao is from Aldona (born January 20, 1953 in Santerxette, Aldona, Goa, India)

St. Thomas Church: the Church of St. Thomas remains an awe inspiring presence in the village of Aldona (estimated population 7000). It was built in 1596 on a high plateau on the banks of the Mapusa River. A flight of broad steps cut into a cliff and lead to an open plain that surrounds the grand white building.

Inside, the Church is ornately decorated by symbolic biblical murals and grand statues. The treasures of the church are the subject of a village legend. At one time, the statues of the church were strung with jewellery by villagers as thanks for prayers answered. But Churches were often robbed of these jewels.

One night, a band of thieves crossed the river into Aldona to rob the Church. At the base of the hill, a young boy appeared to the band's leader and cautioned him not to proceed. The thieves ignored the boy and entered the Church. As they forced open a chest of valuables, the church bells began to ring. Some of the thieves drowned in the river while trying to escape. The leader and some others were captured. When the leader was taken past the main altar, he identified the statue of St. Thomas as the boy he had seen earlier, who warned him not to rob the Church.

Demographics: As of 2001 India census[GRIndia], Aldona had a population of 6320. Males constitute 46% of the population and females 54%. Aldona has an average literacy rate of 79%, higher than the national average of 59.5%; with 49% of the males and 51% of females literate. 9% of the population is under 6 years of age.

Anjuna: Anjuna is a village in Goa, one of the twelve Brahmin comunidades of Bardez. It was a famous destination for hippies during the sixties and seventies. It currently faces the problems that all of Goa faces: garbage disposal, unauthorized land conversion, usurpation of comunidade land, and a disregard for the rule of law.

Its church, founded in 1595, is dedicated to S. Miguel, and celebrates the feasts of S. Miguel (September 29) and Nossa Senhora Advogada (second week of January). There are three large chapels in the parish: the one to S. Antonio (Praias), to Nossa Senhora de Saude (Mazalvaddo), and to Nossa Senhora de Piedade (Grande Chinvar). The chapel at Vagator became the church of the new parish of Vagator, dedicated to S. Antonio, sometime last century.

Anjuna is known throughout North Goa (everything North

of Goa's capital, Panjim) for its Wednesday market, where one can find anything from Indian souvenirs to Trance music.

Aquem

Aquem is a census town in South Goa district in the state of Goa, India.

Demographics: As of 2001 India census[GRIndia], Aquem had a population of 4985. Males constitute 51% of the population and females 49%. Aquem has an average literacy rate of 70%, higher than the national average of 59.5%; with 55% of the males and 45% of females literate. 13% of the population is under 6 years of age.

Baga, Goa

Baga is a beach town in the state of Goa, India. It comes under the jurisdiction of Calangute, which is 2 km (1 mi) south. Baga is known for its white sands, and creek, the Baga Creek. It is visited by thousands of tourists annually.

Bambolim

Bambolim is a census town in North Goa district in the state of Goa, India.

Demographics: As of 2001 India census[GRIndia], Bambolim had a population of 5319. Males constitute 64% of the population and females 36%. Bambolim has an average literacy rate of 82%, higher than the national average of 59.5%; with 69% of the males and 31% of females literate. 10% of the population is under 6 years of age.

Bardez

Bardez is the name of a region in North Goa. The name is credited to the Gaud Saraswat Brahmin immigrants who migrated to the Konkan via Magadha in Gangetic India from Aryavarta, in the north-western part of the Indian sub-continent. Bardez or more properly Bara *desh* means "twelve countries" (or lands). The form "country" probably refers to clan territorial limits, or to the Brahmin comunidades, of which the twelve, in no particular order, are Aldona, Moira, Olaulim, Nachinola, Siolim, Anjuna, Candolim, Serula, Saligao, Sangolda, Assagao, and Pomburpa.

Bardez is delimited on the north by the Chapora River, on the south by the Mandovi River, on the east by the Mapusa River which originates in Bardez itself, near the capital city of Mapusa, and on the west by the Indian Ocean.

A native of Bardez is called a Bardezcar, in the native Konkani language.

Bardez is the site of the legislature of Goa, in the southern village of Britona. Other famous sites are the fort of Aguada, the beaches of Candolim, Sinquerim, Calangute, Baga, Anjuna and Vagator villages, the hill-top monastery and boarding-school of Monte Guirim which was restored by Padre Luna after Pombal's devastation, the village communities of Salvador do Mundo, Penha da Franca, Siolim, Moira, Porvorim, Colvale, Saligao and Sangolda, to name but the most prominent.

The Institute of Hotel Management, Goa and St. Xavier's College are located in Bardez.

The Comunidade of Anjuna was famous as a hippie settlement; among Goans, it is famous as the birthplace of Padre Agnelo Gustavo de Sousa, one of the two most prominent Goan saints, the other being Padre Jose Vas, "Apostle of Sri Lanka".

Benaulim

Benaulim is a beach town a little south of Margao in Goa, India. Benaulim also known as Banavali, is a town of immense natural beauty, located along the scenic south goa coastline. Legend has it that Lord Parashurama, incarnation of Lord Vishnu, shot an arrow from the Sahyadri mountains in adjacent konkan; the arrow (Baan in Sanskrit) landed at the site of this present-day town. The village also host a special significance for christians as it is the birthplace of Father Joseph Vaz.

Bicholim

Bicholim is a town in the territory of Goa, and the headquarters of the consuelho (district) of the same name; the Consuelho of Bicholim, located in the north-east quarter is one of the seven that make up the Novas Conquistas or *New Conquests*, territories added to Goa comparatively latter than the first three of the Velhas Conquistas.

The town is located about 30 kilometres from the capital Ponnjhe. It is in the mining heartland of Goa.

Calangute

Calangute is a census town in North Goa in the state of Goa, India. It is famous for its beach which is visited by domestic and international tourists alike.

The peak tourist season is during Christmas and New Year, and during summers in May. To the north lies Baga, and south Candolim. Calanguate remains hot through the year with little temperature fluctuation. Languages spoken include Konkani, English and Hindi.

Demographics: As of 2001 India census[GRIndia], Calangute had a population of 15,776. Males constitute 54% of the population and females 46%. Calangute has an average literacy rate of 73%, higher than the national average of 59.5%; with male literacy of 78% and female literacy of 67%. 10% of the population is under 6 years of age.

Calapor

Calapor is a census town in North Goa district in the state of Goa, India.

Demographics: As of 2001 India census[GRIndia], Calapor had a population of 11,823. Males constitute 50% of the population and females 50%. Calapor has an average literacy rate of 80%, higher than the national average of 59.5%; with male literacy of 85% and female literacy of 76%. 10% of the population is under 6 years of age.

Carapur

Carapur is a census town in North Goa district in the state of Goa, India.

Demographics: As of 2001 India census[GRIndia], Carapur had a population of 5334. Males constitute 50% of the population and females 50%. Carapur has an average literacy rate of 76%, higher than the national average of 59.5%; with male literacy of 83% and female literacy of 69%. 11% of the population is under 6 years of age.

Chicalim

Chicalim is a census town in South Goa district in the state of Goa, India.

Demographics: As of 2001 India census[GRIndia], Chicalim had a population of 7604. Males constitute 58% of the population and females 42%. Chicalim has an average literacy rate of 81%, higher than the national average of 59.5%; with male literacy of 86% and female literacy of 75%. 10% of the population is under 6 years of age.

Chimbel

Chimbel is a census town in North Goa district in the state of Goa, India.

Demographics: As of 2001 India census[GRIndia], Chimbel had a population of 11,983. Males constitute 51% of the population and females 49%. Chimbel has an average literacy rate of 61%, higher than the national average of 59.5%; with male literacy of 67% and female literacy of 54%. 14% of the population is under 6 years of age.

Chinchinim

Chinchinim is a village and a census town in South Goa district in the state of Goa, India. It lies on the banks of river Sal. It has a predominant catholic population and is dotted with typically Goan mansions and small cottages which are colourful and incorporate all the typical features of a Goan village life.

History: The name Chinchinim is probably derived from Chinchinath the local deity from one of the four temples present in Chinchinim. These temples were destroyed by the Portuguese in 1567. A church dedicated to St. Anne was built in the year 1590 by the Jesuits. It was built by contributions from the Communicated of the village and the neighbouring villages. The church was burnt during the Muslim invasions and the present Our Lady of Hope church was built in the year 1627 which was also burnt during the Maratha invasion in 1739. The repairs were done in the following years.

Demographics: As of 2001 India census[GRIndia], Chinchinim had a population of 7033. Males constitute 47% of the population and females 53%. Chinchinim has an average literacy rate of 75%, higher than the national average of 59.5%; with male literacy of 77% and female literacy of 73%. 9% of the population is under 6 years of age.

Chorao

Chorao is an island along the river Mandovi near Panaji, Goa, India. The island was called *chudamani*, meaning stunning precious stone in Sanskrit. Local legends tell of the islands emerging from the diamonds that were thrown away by Yashoda the mother of Lord Krishna. The Islanders call it *chodan* or *chodna*. It was the Portuguese who called it chorao.

The Portuguese noblemen found the island a pleasurable place to live and hence the name *Ilha dos fidalgos (Island* of noblemen). 10 families of Goud Saraswat Brahmins were amongst the earliest settlers of this island. The island was said to be a place of learning and said to have a University of Sanskrit. According to the *Hindu deities and Temples* by Rui Pereira Gomes, the island had ancient temples of Ganesh, Ravalnath, Bhaukadevi, Mallinath, Bhagwati, Devki, Santa-purush, Narayan, Kanteshwar, Chandeshwar and Dadd-sancol. When the Portuguese began to forcibly Christianize the Goan islands, many Hindus fled chudamani and shifted Hindu idols via Mayem to Naroa and Marcela. The island was Christianised by the Jesuits as they did the Island of Divar and salsette

(Saxti). 'An edict of 1556 saw all the lands, gardens and immovables like gold and silver of the temples of the Island of Chorao, Divar, Vanxim and Jua move over to the Jesuits. The gavnkars were warned to do all under this oath, failing which they would forfeit their properties.' - *Jesuit education in Goa*, by Chares J Borges.

A seminary called the *Real colegio de educacao de chorao* was established in April 1761. A temple of Shri Devaki Krishna Bhumika Mallinath was rebuilt on 11th January, 1934.

Amongst the Christian places of worship is the Church of St Bartholemew. The other church is the Church of Our Lady of Grace. Chorao is also home to the Salim Ali Bird Sancutary. Hindus and Christians live peacefully today on this emerald island.

Colvale

Colvale is a census town in North Goa district in the state of Goa, India.

Demographics: As of 2001 India census[GRIndia], Colvale had a population of 5475. Males constitute 55% of the population and females 45%. Colvale has an average literacy rate of 72%, higher than the national average of 59.5%: male literacy is 74% and, female literacy is 69%. In Colvale, 10% of the population is under 6 years of age.

Curchorem

Curchorem is a city in the South Goa District in India, and is part of the Quepem Taluka, in the State of Goa. It is run by a Municipal Council. The city is self sufficient and has a number of hospitals (including a Government Primary Health Centre), schools, a police station, banks, ATMs, a railway station, good road links, a market, a place of worship, restaurants, a play ground, an electricity station and a theatre.

The city is divided to many vaddos and there is an elected member from each vaddo in the municipality. The population is 25000 people.

Curchorem Cacora

Curchorem Cacora is a city and a municipal council in South Goa district in the state of Goa, India.

Demographics: As of 2001 India census[GRIndia], Curchorem Cacora had a population of 21,398. Males constitute 51% of the population and females 49%.

Curchorem Cacora has an average literacy rate of 74%, higher than the national average of 59.5%: male literacy is 79% and, female literacy is 68%. In Curchorem Cacora, 12% of the population is under 6 years of age.

Curti

Curti is a census town in North Goa district in the state of Goa, India.

Demographics: As of 2001 India census[GRIndia], Curti had a population of 13,070. Males constitute 53% of the population and females 47%. Curti has an average literacy rate of 71%, higher than the national average of 59.5%: male literacy is 75% and, female literacy is 67%. In Curti, 13% of the population is under 6 years of age.

Curtorim

Curtorim is a village in the Indian state of Goa, a former territory of Portugal located on the west coast of India.

Description: Curtorim has a predominantly Catholic population. The village was named by the Portuguese as Curtorim.

Earlier it had been called by various other names. It was called ex Codtary, then it became coddetary, then kardally, cuddtari, and Kuddasthali (Sthali means place).

The Church of St Alex is the main feature of the village. It was built in 1597 and is one of the oldest churches in Goa. It is located in front of a water body (Angoddi Tollem) by the centre of the village. The church was first a chapel church; in 1808 it was converted to a church.

Davorlim

Davorlim is a census town in South Goa district in the state of Goa, India.

Demographics: As of 2001 India census[GRIndia], Davorlim had a population of 10,923. Males constitute 52% of the population and females 48%. Davorlim has an average literacy rate of 73%, higher than the national average of 59.5%: male literacy is 78% and, female literacy is 68%. In Davorlim, 12% of the population is under 6 years of age.

Farmagudi

Farmagudi is a town in Goa, India. It belongs to the Ponda taluka. It is located on a plateau 3 kms from the main Ponda City on the way towards Panjim. It is home to the (GVM's) Higher Secondary School, GVM's College of Commerce & Economics, Ponda Education Society's Higher Secondary School, College and The Goa Engineering College.

Fort Aguada

Fort Aguada is an old, well preserved Portuguese fort standing in Goa, India, on Sinquerim beach, overlooking the vast expanses of Arabian Sea. The fort was constructed in 1612 to guard against the Dutch and the Marathas. It was a reference point for the vessels coming from Europe at that time. This old Portuguese fort stands on the beach south of Candolim, at the shore of the Mandovi river.

A freshwater spring within the fort provided water supply to the ships that used to stop-by. This is how the fort got its name: Aguada = Water. On the fort stands a 4-storey Portuguese lighthouse, erected in 1864 and the oldest of its kind in Asia. A part of the fort is converted to central Jail.

Fort Aguada was the most prized and crucial fort of Portuguese. The fort is so large that it envelops the entire peninsula at the south western tip of Bardez. Built on the mouth of river Mandovi, it was strategically located and was the chief defence of Portuguese against the Dutch and Marathas.

The fort got its name 'Aguada' from the word Aguada (Portuguese for water), because of the three fresh water springs inside it. Built in 1612, it was once the grandstand of 79 cannons, a moat around the fort also protected it.

Fort Aguada Beach Resort

The land around the fort is now owned by The Indian Hotels Co. On the ramparts behind the fort is the *Fort Aguada Beach Resort.* The 5-star-rated hotel, owned by the Tata'sis part of an 88-acre complex overlooking the Arabian Sea is situated on Sinquerim Beach. It is located 18 km from Panaji, Old Goa.

Fort Aguada Beach Resort is composed of a number of villas and cottages, with 130 rooms including 24 Terrace Suites. There are also nine restaurants and nearby beaches. In addition to water sports, there recreational facilities for tennis, squash and mountaineering.

Guirim

Guirim is a census town in North Goa district in the Indian state of Goa.

Demographics: As of 2001 India census[GRIndia], Guirim had a population of 6371. Males constitute 51% of the population and females 49%. Guirim has an average literacy rate of 70%, higher than the national average of 59.5%: male literacy is 75%, and female literacy is 65%. In Guirim, 12% of the population is under 6 years of age.

Loutolim

Legend has it that Goud Saraswat Brahmins formed the settlement of Loutolim when they came to Goa from northern India. The word Loutolim arising from *Lovotollem, is* coined from a combination of the words *Tollem* (pond in Konkani) and a grass *Lovo* found growing in plenty around the pond. The village community was based around the temple of Shree Ramnathi. There were other smaller temples dedicated to Shree Santeri (Shanta durga) in the village. The Jesuits undertook the task of Christianization of Salsette and in 1567 A. D. The captain of Fort Rachol ordered the burning and destruction of all the temples in the village. Many *gaunkars* who wanted to preserve their culture and Hindu religion fled to safer grounds in the Sonde Raja territories across the Zuari river with their idols, most famously the Idol of *shree* Ramnathi in what was later known as the novas conquistas (new conquests). Most of those who chose to remain behind had to become Christian.

The *Saviour of the world* Church was built in Loutolim to look after the spiritual needs of the neo-Christians. Unlike other towns in Salcette and Bardez, where churches were built over the demolished temples, in Loutolim, the plot of land where the old Ramnathi temple stood remained vacant due to some opposition amongst the lotlikars. A new temple of Shree Ramnathi has been rebuilt recently at this spot. The original idol of Shree Ramnathi (see picture) now stands in a 18th century temple of Indo-Portuguese architecture in Bandivade, Ponda, Goa. Today, Loutolim has a mixed population of Hindus and Christians, many of them of Saraswat lineage.

Attractions: Ancestral Goa: A theme park called ancestral Goa has been built in Loutolim also called 'big foot'. The largest known laterite sculpture of Mirabai is present in this theme park.

Miranda Mansion: Old Goan Houses, owned by families such as the Mirandas are sometimes opened for public viewing.

Mapusa

Mapusa also spelt at Mapuca, Mhapsa or Mapsa is a town in North Goa, India. It is situated 13 km north of the capital Panaji. The town is the headquarters of Bardez taluka. It is located on the main highway NH-17, linking Mumbai to Trivandrum. Under Portuguese rule, the town's name was spelt Mapuca.

Mapusa is close to one of the main centres of Goa's tourism industry, with its proximity to the beaches in north Goa. Mapusa's proximity to many beaches in the north makes it a suitable base during the tourist season (October to January). Because it is a mainly commercial town (for locals) with a large resident population, Mapusa has only a limited number of hotels and accommodation.

Mapusa comes alive on Friday, the traditional market day. People from surrounding villages and towns come to Mapusa to sell their wares. This fair has a lot of local flavour (unlike some other tourist-oriented fairs or markets) and specialises in agricultural produce, vegetables, locally-grown fruit, spices, clothes and even plants (mainly during the monsoon planting season).

Mapusa has a tropical climate with temperatures ranging from a high of 37 °C in summer with high levels of humidity to a low of 21 °C in winters.

Margao

Margao is also called Madgaon. It is Goa's second largest but busiest town, the commercial capital of the state, and the administrative headquarters of South Goa District and of the Salcete Taluka.

The name may be pronounced as 'Maudgao' in Konkani, the local language. Margao is the Portuguese form, and the form Margao is also common. It is derived from *Mathagram* which means a place with a matha.

Nestled on the banks of the River Sal, Margao is amongst the oldest recorded towns in Goa. Margao is famous for the huge Portuguese style mansions which dot its landscape. It is also one of the fastest growing cities in Goa and includes several suburbs including Aquem, Fatorda, Gogol, Borda, Comba, Davorlim and Fatorda.

Transport: The Margao Railway station is Goa's biggest and most important as it is a railway junction positioned at the intersection of the Konkan Railway and the South Western Railway. All trains passing through Goa stop here, and it is the gateway to south Goa. Hence Margao is used more commonly as a transit stop rather than as a tourist destination, by many people who either head off down south to Palolem (38 km) or to Benaulim and Colva which are about six kilometers away.

Tourism: The city has many sights and destinations. These include the 'Closed' Market called, in the Portuguese language, *Mercado de Afonso de Albuquerque* or in Konkani as "Pimplapedd" or "Pimpalakatta," the municipal building (*Câmara*), the muncipal garden, Anna Fonte (natural springs), Old Market or *Mercado Velho*, Holy Spirit Church, grand colonial mansions, the view and chapel at Monte Hill, the Hindu crematorium or 'Smashant' and the Muslim burial ground or 'Kabrasthan' both situated on Pajifond's *Rua das Saudades*.

Some of the city suburbs include Pajifond, Aquem, Gogol, Borda, Malbhat, Kharebandh, Old Market, Navelim and Comba, the last two being the oldest parts of the city.

The many temples in Margao, 1) The 'Damodar Temple'(Saal) is in the house of Naik Family and is famed as place where Swami Vivekanand stayed for a while before departing for Chicago to attend Parliament of Religion, 2) The 'Hari Mandir' is located in Malbhat, 3) 'Maruti Mandir' at Davorlim and other in Comba, 'Saibaba Temple' at Davorlim, 4) The 'Shiv Temple '(Ling) at Fatorda near Nehru Stadium.

Educational Instituitions: Margao hosts many prestigious schools and colleges. Among the schools known for excellence is Loyola High School. It is run by the Jesuits 'SJ' of Goa. It is an all boy's school known for producing some of Goa's most famous son's and students who excel both in academics and in sports.

Though the town is also known as the cultural capital of Goa, a culture centre ('Ravindra Bhavan') is still under construction at Fatorda. It also has Goa's only sports stadium, the Nehru Stadium at Fatorda and hosts the test track for Skybus, an elevated rail system which is patented by the Konkan Railway Corporation.

History: Margao in pre-Portuguese times was one of the important settlements in Salcete and known as *Matha Grama* (the village of Mathas) as it was a temple town with nine

Mathas in temple schools. Most of the inhabitant were Brahmin. It was then famous for its many outstanding and beautifully built temples, and long before the Portuguese came it had a university with a library.

During the Portuguese conquest in 1543 Hindu temples were demolished and Catholic churches were built in their place. Almost all traces of Hindu settlements were wiped out. The first church to be built in Margao, and its replacement in 1579, were destroyed by raiders along with the seminary that had been built along side. The present church was built in 1675.

The initial settlement of Margao grew from the site of the Holy Spirit church. The original temple here was demolished and the temple tank filled up to be replaced by the church and church grounds that came up in its place. While the western side developed as a market place the settlement grew on the eastern side, that is, the Borda region. The settlement grew with the church at its core and extended outwards.

Margao's importance as an administrative and commercial area grew with the increasing dependence of the surrounding towns and villages; leading to the administrative centre with the town hall at its centre being built in the south. The commercial market became attached to it and was hence called *maud-gao* or the market town of Goa, and since then the city has grown towards the east.

The Holy Spirit main square is defined on one side by the church with its baroque architecture and the parochial house, and on the other side by the palatial mansions of affluent elite Catholics, positioned in a row. The *Associacao das Communidades* building and the school being the odd exceptions. They add to its character and sense of scale. They have a maximum height of two stories, and *balcoes* (singular: *balcao*) and *varandas* facing the square. Parallel to the church square is the commercial street (old market). There is also a landscaped area next to the church called *Praca da Alegria* (meaning: joy square).

Some lesser known information about some famous landmarks: Margao municipal garden: The northern segment of the Margao municipal garden was developed by the Mavany family and is named after Aga Khan, during his visit just before Goa's liberation. The entire garden is now Municipal property and is maintained by the Margao Municipal Council.

Narcinva D. Naik residence/Damodar Sal: Swami Vivekananda stayed in this house during his visit to Goa in October 1892. The mansion also houses Margao's well-known temple-hall "Damodar Bal Sunner".

Mormugao

Mormugao is a city and a municipal council in South Goa district in the Indian state of Goa. It is Goa's main port. Its appearance in the 1980 film The Sea Wolves is one of its few global advertisements, but it has a fascinating past. When the Portuguese colonised part of Goa in the sixteenth century, they based their operations in the central district of Tiswadi, notably in the international emporium City of Goa, now Old Goa. As threats to their maritime supremacy increased, they built forts on various hillocks, especially along the coast. In 1624 they began to build their fortified town on the headland overlooking Mormugao harbour.

The sultans of Bijapur, who had colonised Goa before the Portuguese, did not give up easily. There were several invasions. From the sea came the Dutch, who eventually took over from the Portuguese most of the coastal settlements: the Moluccas, Batticaloa, Trincomali, Galle, Malacca, Manar, Jaffna, Quilon, Cochin and Cannanore. From 1640 to 1643, the Dutch tried their best to capture Mormugao but were finally driven away.

In 1683, the Portuguese in Goa were in grave danger from the Marathas. Almost certain defeat was averted when Sambhaji suddenly lifted siege and rushed to defend his own kingdom from the Mughal Aurangzeb. The narrow escape, no less than the decline of the City of Goa, convinced the Portuguese viceroy, Dom Francisco de Tavora, that he should shift the capital of the Portuguese holdings in India to Mormugao's formidable fortress.

In 1685 the new city's principle edifices were under construction, with the Jesuit priest Father Teotonio Rebelo in charge. The Jesuit architects made a consistent effort to avoid the ornate style of the time.

The austere viceregal palace still stands, having been used, after its short stint as a palace, in various capacities, including as the hotel which housed the British agents who in 1943 destroyed German ships anchored in Mormugao's neutral waters.

Viceroys after Tavora found Mormugao too secluded for their liking. The administrative headquarters were moved to the new city of Panjim, which is till today Goa's chief city.

Epidemics devastated Mormugao during the eighteenth century, but after that its fortunes turned. As the importance of one of India's best natural harbours grew more apparent, Mormugao, which the British called Marmagoa, became a key trading point.

It was chosen for the terminus of the new railway linking the Portuguese colony to British India. For a fabulous price, the Western India Portuguese Guaranteed Railways Company, a British enterprise, modernised the port and built the railway. Both were opened to the public in July 1886.

Mormugao's city of Vasco da Gama was planned and built in the early years of the twentieth century. A colourful city of officials, traders and migrant labourers, it had its Portuguese academies and British club life for several decades. Now rather scarred, Mormugao district continues to be unique in Goa. With Goa's airport at Dabolim, the railway terminus at Vasco da Gama, and the busy port, Mormugao is many visitors' first experience of Goa.

Demographics: As of 2001 India census[GRIndia], Mormugao had a population of 97,085. Males constitute 53% of the population and females 47%. Mormugao has an average literacy rate of 75%, higher than the national average of 59.5%: male literacy is 80%, and female literacy is 70%. In Mormugao, 11% of the population is under 6 years of age.

Panaji

Panaji is the capital of the Indian state of Goa. It lies on the banks of the Mandovi estuary, in the district of North Goa. With a population of 65,000 (a metropolitan population of 100,000 if suburbs are included), Panaji is Goa's third largest city after Vasco and Margao.

The current official name is *Panaji*. The Portuguese name was *Pangim*. The city is called *Panjim* in English. It has been spelt as *Panaji* since the 1960s, and is also called *Ponnje* in Konkani, the widely spoken local language.

Earlier a small village on the riverfront, in 1843 the city had been renamed *Nova Goa* (Portuguese for *New Goa*) when it officially replaced the city of Goa (now Old Goa) as the administrative seat of Portuguese India, though the viceroy had already moved there in 1759.

After the end of Portuguese colonial rule, it was incorporated with the rest of Goa and the former Portuguese colonies, into India in December 1961.

Panaji became a state-capital on Goa's elevation to statehood in May 1987. Between 1961 and 1987, it was the capital of the Union Territory of Goa, Daman and Diu.

A new Legislative Assembly complex was inaugurated in March 2000, across the Mandovi river, in the suburb of Porvorim. Panaji is also the administrative headquarters of North Goa district.

The heart of the city is the Church Square or Municipal Garden with the Portuguese Baroque *Our Lady of the Immaculate Conception* Church, originally built in 1541.

Other tourist attractions include the old and rebuilt Adilshahi Palace (or *Idalcao* palace), dating from the 16th century, the Menezes Braganza Institute and the Central Library, the*Mahalaxmi* Temple, the *Jama Masjid* mosque, the Chapel of St. Sebastian and the Fontainhas area in general which is considered to be the Old Latin Quarter, as well as the nearby beach of Miramar. The Carnival celebrations in February include a colourful parade on the streets. This is followed by the Shigmo, a local Hindu spring festival.

Welknown places in Panaji are the 18th June Road (a busy thoroughfare in the heart of town and a shopping area for tourists and locals), Mala area, Miramar beach and the Kala Academy cultural centre known for its structure built by famous architect Charles Correa. Kala Academy in Panaji is a place where Goa showcases its culture and art.

6

Economy

Goa's state domestic product for 2017 is estimated at $11 billion at current prices. Goa is India's richest state with the highest GDP per capita – two and a half times that of the country – with one of its fastest growth rates: 8.23% (yearly average 1990–2000). Tourism is Goa's primary industry: it gets 12% of foreign tourist arrivals in India. Goa has two main tourist seasons: winter and summer. In winter, tourists from abroad (mainly Europe) come, and summer (which, in Goa, is the rainy season) sees tourists from across India. Goa's net state domestic product (NSDP) was around US$7.24 billion in 2015–16.

The land away from the coast is rich in minerals and ores, and mining forms the second largest industry. Iron, bauxite, manganese, clays, limestone and silica are mined. The Mormugao port handled 31.69 million tonnes of cargo last year, which was 39% of India's total iron ore exports. Sesa Goa (now owned by Vedanta Resources) and Dempo are the lead miners. Rampant mining has been depleting the forest cover as well as posing a health hazard to the local population. Corporations are also mining illegally in some areas. During 2015–16, the total traffic handled by Mormugao port was recorded to be 20.78 million tones.

Agriculture, while of shrinking importance to the economy over the past four decades, offers part-time employment to a sizeable portion of the populace. Rice is the main agricultural crop, followed by areca, cashew and coconut. Fishing employs about 40,000 people, though recent official figures indicate a decline of the importance of this sector and also a fall in catch, due perhaps, to traditional fishing giving way to large-scale mechanised trawling.

Gross State Domestic Product (in millions of Rupees)

Year	GSDP
1980	3,980
1985	6,550
1990	12,570
1995	33,190
2000	76,980
2010	150,000

Train carrying iron ore to MarmagaoPort, Vasco

Medium scale industries include the manufacturing of pesticides, fertilisers, tyres, tubes, footwear, chemicals, pharmaceuticals, wheat products, steel rolling, fruits and fish canning, cashew nuts, textiles, brewery products.

Currently there are 16 planned SEZs in Goa. The Goa government has recently decided to not allow any more special economic zones (SEZs) in Goa after strong opposition to them by political parties and the powerful Goa Catholic Church.

Commercial area in Panaji

Goa is also notable for its low priced beer, wine and spirits prices due to its very low excise duty on alcohol. Another main source of cash inflow to the state is remittance, from many of its citizens who work abroad, to their families. It is said to have some of the largest bank savings in the country.

Goa is the second state in India to achieve a 100 per cent automatic telephone system with a solid network of telephone exchanges. As of September 2017, Goa had a total installed power generation capacity of 547.88 MW. Goa is also one of the few states in India to achieve 100 per cent rural electrification.

TRANSPORTATION

Air

Goa International Airport, is a civil enclave at INS Hansa,

a Naval airfield located at Dabolim near Vasco da Gama. The airport caters to scheduled domestic and international air services.

Goa International Airport, new terminal building

Goa has scheduled international connections to Doha, Dubai, Muscat, Sharjah and Kuwaitin the Middle East by airlines like Air Arabia, Air India, GoAir, Indigo, Oman Air, SpiceJet, Jet Airways, JetKonnect and Qatar Airways. The proposed greenfield Mopa Airport will be built at Mopa in Pernem taluka.

Road

Most of Goa is well connected by roads

Government-run Kadamba buses at a bus station in Goa

Goa's public transport largely consists of privately operated buses linking the major towns to rural areas. Government-run buses, maintained by the Kadamba Transport Corporation, link major routes (like the Panaji–Margao route) and some remote parts of the state.

The Corporation owns 15 bus stands, 4 depots and one Central workshop at Porvorim and a Head Office at Porvorim. In large towns such as Panajiand Margao, intra-city buses operate.

However, public transport in Goa is less developed, and residents depend heavily on their own transportation, usually motorised two-wheelers and small family cars.

Motorcycle Taxi or "Pilots"

Goa has four National Highways passing through it. NH-66 (ex NH-17) runs along India's west coast and links Goa to Mumbai in the north and Mangalore to the south.

NH-4A running across the state connects the capital Panaji to Belgaum in east, linking Goa to cities in the Deccan. The NH-366 (ex NH-17A) connects NH-66 to Mormugao Port from Cortalim. The new NH-566 (ex NH-17B) is a four-lane highway connecting Mormugao Port to NH-66 at Verna via Dabolim Airport, primarily built to ease pressure on the NH-366 for traffic to Dabolim Airport and Vasco da Gama.

NH-768 (ex NH-4A) links Panaji and Ponda to Belgaum and NH-4. Goa has a total of 224 km (139 mi) of national highways, 232 km (144 mi) of state highway and 815 kilometres

(506 miles) of district highway. National Highways in Goa are among the narrowest in the country and will remain so for the foreseeable future, as the state government has received an exemption that allows narrow national highways. In Kerala, highways are 45 metres (148 feet) wide. In other states National Highways are grade separated highways 60 metres (200 feet) wide with a minimum of four lanes, as well as 6 or 8 lane access-controlled expressways.

Hired forms of transport include unmetered taxis and, in urban areas, auto rickshaws. Another form of transportation in Goa is the motorcycle taxi, operated by drivers who are locally called "pilots". These vehicles transport a single pillion rider, at fares that are usually negotiated. Other than buses, "pilots" tend to be the cheapest mode of transport. River crossings in Goa are serviced by flat-bottomed ferry boats, operated by the river navigation department.

Rail

Margao railway station

Goa has two rail lines – one run by the South Western Railway and the other by the Konkan Railway. The line run by the South Western Railway was built during the colonial era linking the port town of Vasco da Gama, Goa with Belgaum, Hubli, Karnataka via Margao. The Konkan Railway line, which was built during the 1990s, runs parallel to the coast connecting major cities on the western coast.

Sea

The Mormugao harbour near the city of Vasco handles mineral ore, petroleum, coal, and international containers. Much of the shipments consist of minerals and ores from Goa's hinterland.

Panaji, which is on the banks of the Mandovi, has a minor port, which used to handle passenger steamers between Goa and Mumbai till the late 1980s. There was also a short-lived catamaran service linking Mumbai and Panaji operated by Damania Shipping in the 1990s.

7

Tourism

Tourism is generally focused on the coastal areas of Goa, with decreased tourist activity inland. In 2010, there were more than 2 million tourists reported to have visited Goa, about 1.2 million of whom were from abroad. As of 2013, Goa was a destination of choice for Indian and foreign tourists, particularly Britons and Russians, with limited means who wanted to party. The state was hopeful that changes could be made which would attract a more upscale demographic.

International and Indian tourists visit Goa

Goa stands 6th in the Top 10 Nightlife cities in the world in National Geographic Travel. One of the biggest tourist attractions in Goa is water sports. Beaches like Baga and Calangute offer jet-skiing, parasailing, banana boat rides, water scooter rides, and more. Patnem beach in Palolem stood 3rd in CNN Travel's Top 20 Beaches in Asia. Over 450 years of Portuguese rule and the influence of the Portuguese culture presents to visitors to Goa a cultural environment that is not found elsewhere in India. Goa is often described as a fusion between Eastern and Western culture with Portuguese culture having a dominant position in the state be it in its architectural, cultural or social settings. The state of Goa is famous for its excellent beaches, churches, and temples. The Bom Jesus Cathedral, Fort Aguada and a new wax museum on Indian history, culture and heritage in Old Goa are other tourism destinations.

Historic sites and neighbourhoods

Goa has two World Heritage Sites: the Bom Jesus Basilica and churches and convents of Old Goa. The basilica holds the mortal remains of St. Francis Xavier, regarded by many Catholics as the patron saint of Goa (the patron of the Archdiocese of Goa is actually Saint Joseph Vaz). These are both Portuguese-era monuments and reflect a strong European character. The relics are taken down for veneration and for public viewing, as per the prerogative of the Church in Goa, not every ten or twelve years as popularly thought and propagated. The last exposition was held in 2014.

Our Lady of Immaculate ConceptionChurch in Panaji

Tourist Arrivals

Year	Total Arrivals	% Change
1985	775,212	
1990	881,323	13.3
1995	1,107,705	23.7
2000	1,268,513	13.8
2005	2,302,146	66.3
2010	2,644,805	13.9
2015	5,297,902	76.4

Goa has the Sanctuary of Saint Joseph Vaz in Sancoale. Pilar monastery which holds novenas of Venerable Padre Agnelo Gustavo de Souza from 10 November to 20 November yearly. There is a claimed Marian Apparition at the Church of Saints Simon and Jude at Batim, Ganxim, near Pilar, where Goans and non-resident Goans visit. There is the statue of the bleeding Jesus on the Crucifix at the Santa Monica Convent in Velha Goa. There are churches (*Igorzo*), like the Baroque styled *Nixkollounk Gorb-Sombhov Saibinnich Igorz* (Church of the Our Lady of Immaculate Conception) in Panaji, the Gothic styled *Mater Dei* (*Dêv Matechi Igorz*/ Mother of God) church in Saligao and each church having its own style and heritage, besides *Kopelam / Irmidi* (chapels).

The Velhas Conquistas regions are known for Goa-Portuguese style architecture. There are many forts in Goa such as Tiracol, Chapora, Corjuem, Aguada, Reis Magos, Nanus, Mormugao, Fort Gaspar Dias and Cabo de Rama.

In many parts of Goa, mansions constructed in the Indo-Portuguese style architecture still stand, though in some villages, most of them are in a dilapidated condition. Fontainhas in Panaji has been declared a cultural quarter, showcasing the life, architecture and culture of Goa. Influences from the Portuguese era are visible in some of Goa's temples, notably the Shanta Durga Temple, the Mangueshi Temple, the Shri Damodar Temple and the Mahalasa Temple. After 1961, many of these were demolished and reconstructed in the indigenous Indian style.

Museums and science centre

Goa has three important museums: the Goa State Museum, the Naval Aviation Museum and the National Institute of Oceanography. The aviation museum is one of three in India (the others are in Delhi and Bengaluru). The Goa Science Centre is in Miramar, Panaji. The National Institute of Oceanography (NIO) is in Dona Paula.

8

Population and Religion

POPULATION OF GOA 2018

Goa is a state located in southwest piece of India, bordered by Maharashtra and Karnataka, while the Arabian Sea shapes its western coast. It is India's smallest state as far as region and the fourth smallest in terms of population. Goa is one of India's wealthiest states with a GDP per capita more than two times that of the country.

It was ranked the best placed state by the Eleventh Finance Commission for its system and situated on top for the best personal fulfilment in India by the National Commission on Population considering the 12 Indicators. Panaji is the capital and Vasco da Gama is the biggest city.

Population Of Goa In 2018

There are 394 individuals for every square kilometre of area which is higher than national normal 382 per square km. It is the state with most noteworthy extent of urban population with 62.17% of the population living in urban ranges.

Talking about population, in order to check out the population of Goa in 2018, we need to have a look at the population of the past 5 years. They are as per the following:

1. 2013 – 1.88 Million

2. 2014 – 2.30 Million
3. 2015 – 2.68 Million
4. 2016 – 2.89 Million
5. 2017 – 3.1046 Million

Predicting the 2018 population of Goa is not easy but we can get the idea after analysing the population from the year 2013 – 17. As we have seen that every year the population increases by approximate 0.24492 Million people. Hence, the population of Goa in 2018 is forecast to be 3.1046 Million + 0.24492 Million = 3.34952 Million. So, the population of Goa in the year 2018 as per estimated data is 3.34952 Million.

Goa Population 2018 –3.34952 Million. (estimated).

Demography Of Goa

As showed by the 2011 measurements, in a population of 1,458,545 people, 66. % were Hindu, 26% Christian and 8.3% Muslim. Different minorities of around 0.1% comprised of Sikhism, Jainism and Buddhism. The sex proportion is 973 females to 1000 males. The birth rate is 15.70 for each 1,000 people in 2007. Goa in like manner is the state with most reduced extent of Scheduled Tribes at 0.04%.

Population Density And Growth Of Goa

The population density is 394 persons per square kilometre. The population has a growth rate of 8.23% consistently. In the two decades that took after Goa's freedom, its population growth got pace with a rise by 34% in the 70's and 26% in the 80's. Regardless, it has quite recently been a slipping example. As demonstrated by the latest data released under list 2011, its population has grown just by 8.23% since the 2001 enlistment.

This is the most insignificant population growth that Goa has found in the latest 40 years. From 1961 to 1971, the population rate was 34.77%. It declined to 26.74% something close to 1971 and 1981 and to 16% around 1981 and 1991.

Dropping fertility rates and the mortality odometer swinging reverse, its young workforce moving a long way from its shores and the extending example of the state being a top place for the country's elderly citizens emit an impression of simply adding to Goa's developing population.

Facts About Goa:

1. The export of mineral metal began during the sixteenth century here in Goa.

2. Goa's Naval Aviation Museum is novel and Asia's first. There are simply around six other such exhibitions on the planet.

3. The Goa Medical College was the nation's first medicinal school setup to teach imminent specialists and to offer medications.

4. Goa has a shocking number of bars. Out and out, there are around 7000 bars and each one of them are approved to serve alcohol.

5. Individuals living and working in the state have a huge amount of money to spare.

DEMOGRAPHICS

Population

Population growth

Census	Pop.	%±
1951	547,000	—
1961	590,000	7.9%
1971	795,000	34.7%
1981	1,008,000	26.8%
1991	1,170,000	16.1%
2001	1,347,668	15.2%
2011	1,731,031	28.4%

A native of Goa is called a Goan. Goa has a population of 1.459 million residents, making it India's fourth smallest (after Sikkim, Mizoram and Arunachal Pradesh). The population has a growth rate of 8.23% per decade. There are 394 people for each square kilometre of land which is higher than national average 382 per km. Goa is the state with highest proportion of urban population with 62.17% of the population living in urban areas. The sex ratio is 973 females to 1,000 males. The birth rate is 15.70 per 1,000 people in 2007. Goa also is the state with lowest proportion of Scheduled Tribes at 0.04%. A relatively small Goan-Portuguese mixed race population resulted from Portuguese colonization, one estimate being that less than 100 mestiço families left in 1961 when Portugal lost the colony.

Languages

Konkani	57%
Marathi	23%
Hindi	5.7%
Kannada	5.5%
Urdu	4.0%
Others	4.8%

The Goa, Daman and Diu Official Language Act, 1987 makes Konkani in the Devanagari script the sole official language of Goa, but provides that Marathi may also be used "for all or any of the official purposes". Portuguese was the sole official language during Portuguese colonial rule. It is now, however, mostly spoken by only the elderly Portuguese-educated populations and is no longer an official language.The Government also has a policy of replying in Marathi to correspondence received in Marathi. Whilst there have been demands for according Konkani in the Roman script official status in the state, there is widespread support for keeping Konkani as the sole official language of Goa. It is however notable to mention that the entire liturgy and communication of the Catholic church in Goa is done solely in the Roman script of Konkani.

Konkani is spoken as a native language by about 57% of the people in the state but almost all Goans can speak and understand Konkani. Other linguistic minorities in the state as per the 2001 census are speakers of Marathi (23%), Kannada (5.5%), Hindi (5.7%), and Urdu (4%).

Until 1987, Konkani was neither the official nor administrative language used by the various rulers of the State. Under the Kadambas (c. 960 – 1310) the court language was Kannada, a Dravidian language, and when under Muslim rule (1312-1370 and 1469-1510), the official and cultural language was Persian; various stones in the Goa Archaeological Museum from the period are inscribed in Kannada and Persian. During the intervening periods of Muslim rule, the Vijayanagara control of the State mandated the use of Telugu, another Dravidian language.

RELIGION

Hindu-Christianity Unity Memorial at Miramar Beach.

Religion in Goa (2011)

Hinduism (66.08%)

Christianity (25.10%)

Islam (8.33%)

Sikhism (0.10%)

Buddhism (0.08%)

Jainism (0.08%)

Other or not religious (0.2%)

According to the 2011 census, in a population of 1,458,545 people, 66.1% were Hindu, 25.1% were Christian, and 8.3% were Muslim. Smaller minorities of about 0.1% each followed Sikhism, Buddhism, or Jainism.

Due to the economic decline of the Estado da India from the eighteenth century, there was a large scale migration of Goan Catholics. The local Indian Christians were called "indiacatos" and the mixed population, mestiços by the Portuguese. The population moved from 64.5% Christians and 35% Hindus in 1851 to 50% Christians and 50% Hindus in 1900, with a steady increase in the Hindu proportion from then onwards. The Catholics in Goa state and Daman and Diu union territory are served by the Metropolitan Roman Catholic Archdiocese of Goa and Daman, the primatial see of India, in which the titular Patriarchate of the East Indies is vested.

Religions in Goa

Goans are deeply pious people and religion play an important role in the Goan society. Hinduism and Christianity are the two major religions in Goa, together constituting around 95% of the population. The Goan society epitomizes the ethos of religious tolerance and despite the bitter memories of the Inquisition, people with different religious persuasions have peacefully co-existed throughout the ages.

Hinduism

Hinduism is the dominant religion in Goa. A large number of prominent Hindu temples scatter across the length and breadth of Goa. The long rule of the Portuguese tried to crush the Hindus with widespread destruction of temples and forcefully converting thousands of Hindus. But Hinduism still survived in Goa and devotees clandestinely carried on worshipping their deities in makeshift temples. Ponda is regarded the cradle of Hinduism in Goa and there is a profusion of sacred Hindu temples in and around Goa.

Christianity

Christianity arrived on the Goan shores courtesy the priests accompanying the traders from Portugal. The missionaries preached Christianity and also contributed to the development of the native Konkani language. During the Inquisition, thousands of locals were converted to Christianity and that period witnessed a proliferation of churches in Goa. Besides being prominent religious institutions, churches play a prominent role in Goa's social fabric.

Islam

Goa has a minuscule Muslim population. During the reign of Sultan Adil Shah of Bijapur, Goa witnessed a proliferation of mosques and other Islamic monuments. The Safa Shahouri mosque in Ponda is the biggest mosque in Goa. The Muslim community in Goa celebrates their traditional festivals with religious fervor and devotion.

CHRISTIANITY IN GOA

Christianity is the second largest religious grouping in Goa, India. According to the 2011 census, 25% of the population are Christian, while 66% are Hindu. The Christian population is almost entirely Roman Catholic, and Goan Catholics form a significant ethnoreligious group. There is a higher proportion of Christians in Velhas Conquistas than in Novas Conquistas.

History: (Possibility of) Pre-Portuguese Christianity in Goa

Christianity in Goa has pre-Portuguese roots, according to

a few scholars such as H.O. Mascarenhas and Jose Cosme Costa. These roots are probably the same as those of the Saint Thomas Christians or Nasranis of Kerala. Christianity, here at this time, was believed to be spread by Saint Thomas and/or Saint Bartholomew who preached in the Malabar and Konkan coasts respectively.

Evidence

1. The metallic crucifix found in a wall of a house at Old Goa by Afonso de Albuquerque, a few days after the conquest of Tiswadi in November 1510. A road was later named after this crucifix — "Rua de Crucifixo". #The document of a gift (*doação*) on a metallic plate given to a "pagoda" of Goa Velha by a Hindu king in 1391 which speaks of Trinity and divine incarnation, and later produced in the court of the city of Old Goa in 1532.
2. Ibn Batuta's testimony that in 1342 AD, he found Christian settlements on the banks of the River Agashini (river Zuari).
3. The *Saint Thomas Cross* with Pahlavi inscription found by Fr J. Cosme Costa on the banks of the river Zuari.
4. An article in the *Examiner* (Bombay) on Pre-Portuguese Christianity which speaks of Thomas crosses on the Hill of Colvale (Bardez) which people would hide in olden days, fearing their destruction by the Portuguese.

Portuguese rule

After the Portuguese Conquest of Goa in 1510 and its subsequent rule by Portugal, Goa's indigenous population underwent a large-scale conversion to Christianity.

The state of Goa became the center of Christianisation in the east. The evangelisation activities of Goa was divided in 1555 by the Portuguese viceroy of Goa, Pedro Mascarenhas. He allotted Bardez to the Franciscans, Tiswadi to the Dominicans, and Salcette, together with fifteen southeastern villages of Tiswadi, including Chorão and Divar, to the Jesuits.

Chapel of St. Catherine, built in Old Goa during the Portuguese occupation. It should not be confused with the Cathedral of Santa Catarina, also in Old Goa.

After conversion, locals were usually granted Portuguese citizenship. The rapid rise of converts in Goa has been described as mostly the result of Portuguese economic and political control over the Hindus, who were vassals of the Portuguese crown.

The process of Christianisation was simultaneously accompanied by "Lusitanisation", as the Christian converts typically assumed a Portuguese veneer. This was most visible by the discarding of old Hindu names for new Christian Portuguese names. Converts usually adopted the surnames of the Portuguese priest, governor, soldier or layman who stood as godfather for their baptism ceremony. For instance, the *Boletim do Instituto Vasco da Gama* lists the new names of some of the prominent *ganvkars* (Konkani: Freeholders):

Rama Prabhu, the son of Dado Vithal Prabhu from Benaulim, Salcette became Francisco Fernandes, while Mahabal Pai, the son of Nara Pai, became Manuel Fernandes in 1596. Mahabal Kamati of Curtorim became Aleisco Menezes in 1607, while Chandrappa Naik of Gandaulim became António Dias in 1632. In 1595, Vittu Prabhu became Irmao de Diego Soares and the son of Raulu Kamat became Manuel Pinto in Aldona, Bardez. Ram Kamat of Punola became Duarte Lobo in 1601, while Tados Irmaose of Anjuna became João de Souza in 1658.

However, the converted Hindus retained their mother tongue (which in most cases, was Konkani) and caste status, even after becoming Christian. Based on their previous caste affiliations, the new converts were usually lumped into their new respective Catholic castes. The converts from the priestly Brahmin class were *Bamonns* (Konkani word for Brahmins). All converted Brahmins were lumped into the Christian caste of *Bamonn*. The converts from the Kshatriya caste who formed the second largest group were *Chardos* (Konkani word for Kshatriya); and converts from the labour class Shudra which formed the largest group became *Sudirs* (Konkani word for Shudra).

The Portuguese demolished almost all the temples from the Velhas conquests.The temple art, along with its literature was destroyed, as a part of the Christianisation initiatives by the Portuguese. But these temples and their idols were relocated in other places in Goa, especially in the Novas conquistas.

Goa inquisition

In 1560, the Inquisition established an office in Goa. It was finally abolished in 1812. It involved persecution of Hindus as well as Christians deemed not compatible with the Latin rite of Christianity. However, it accounted a very poor activity.

Modern times

Since 1851, the Christian population of Goa has been facing a continual decline. This is caused by an emigration of Goan Catholics from Goa, to other places in India and abroad, as well as, large waves of Hindu immigrants from the rest of India. As a result, the percentage of Christian population (once a majority) has shifted in favour of the Hindus. As per the data available, Christians constituted 64% and Hindus 35% in 1851 census. Currently, Christians constitute 27% and Hindus 66% of the population of Goa.

In 2001, the Goan Konkani New Testament was being re-translated. According to *Operation World*, the old translation is "little understood today."

Roman Catholicism

The Archbishop of the Roman Catholic Archdiocese of Goa and Daman carries the title Patriarch of the East Indies. Old Goa was once called "Rome of the East" and was the capital of the Roman church in the eastern world. The remains of the Jesuit St. Francis Xavier are kept in veneration in the Basílica de Bom Jesus. The Sé Catedral de Santa Catarina is one of the largest church buildings in Asia. The Igreja de São Francisco de Assis, built in 1661, now houses an archaeological museum. Plenty of churches can be seen all over the state with impressive Portuguese-Baroque architecture. Goa used to once be a hotspot for priestly vocations, though that no longer the case. The Goan Catholics still prefer the read Konkani in its Latin script rather than its Devanagiri counterpart, especially during the liturgy.

RELIGIOUS PRACTICES

Sacraments among Hindus

The Samskaras (sacraments) begin to be observed right from the day of conception signaled by Garbhadana or conception of foetus in the womb of the woman. Usually the birth of the first child has to take place in the woman's mothers home called kular in konkani. Before the woman is sent to her mothers home, a ceremony known as fulam malop (adorn the coiffure with flowers) is held in the 5th, 7th and 9th months of pregnancy. The first two flower-bedecking are held at the husband's house. In the 5th month, her lap is filled with green clothes.

On the sixth day from the birth of the child there is a ceremony called Sotti or Shastipujan. On that night there is the honouring of the female deity called Sottvai and the whole night resounds to the beat of the 'ghumott', which is a special local percussion instrument made from a mud-pot.

A ten day's period of seclusion is observed when the woman just delivered, is prevented from touching things that matter. On the 11th day, the delivered woman is bathed and offered panchagavya consisting of cow's urine, tulsi leaves, cow-dung etc. 'Homa' is held and water from the tulsi plant is brought into the house and sprinkled on house-hold things for the purpose of purification and the delivered woman given an offering of coconut, sweet preparation in liquid-paste form called godshem, puris, rice, moong etc. The umbilical cord is buried in some place in the backyard.

On the twelfth day the child's Barso *i.e.* the naming ceremony is performed. Married women (with husbands living) meet and fill up the lap of the delivered woman with flowers and gifts. The child is placed in the cradle and bestowed a name. Normally, three names including a surname are given. The first being the proper name of the boy or girl, the second being the father's name and the third being the surname.

When the child cuts its first tooth, there is a function to celebrate the occasion with food etc. This is known as datolem ghalop (cutting of tooth). Little puris, biscuits and items of snacks are strewn over the head of the child and distributed to the children gathered all around. This practice is on the decline these days. Wherever it is prevalent the Vodde (puri-type) have been replaced by chocolate, toffee, peppermint etc.

Munj or Upanayana is done among the Saraswats, Daivednya (goldsmiths), Vanis, Kshatriya, etc. It is not done among the Sudra communities. Formerly the Upanayana used to be performed between the ages of 8 and 10. Marriages do not take place before the performance of the Munj ceremony. Munj has sometimes to be performed on the eve of the marriage. Upanayana was meant to usher in the period of education of a student.

The last Samskara among the Hindus is the funeral rite or Antyesti at the death of a person. After the death of a person, a period of 12 days mourning observance is adhered to. On the 10th day after death, a homa is prepared at home and panchagavya done for purification. On the 12th day, there is the Baravo on which day there is the performance of the Shraddha Vidhan ceremony of the passing away of the person concerned and offerings are given to the public and food to the priests. There used to be a practice to have the Shraddha as bharni-shraddha, monthly Shraddha and yearly Shraddha. Now only the annual Shraddha is observed.

Sacraments among Christians

The sacraments among the Christians is same as the sacraments performed by the Christians elsewhere. The sacrament performed by the Goan Christians are Baptism, Holy communion, Confirmation, Ordination, Marriage and Extreme unction.

Sacraments among Muslims

A special feature of the Muslim sacraments, is that they can be performed without the presence of the priest or Mullah, when they are not available for some reason or another.

Paidaish is the first sacrament, which concerns the birth of a child. The first delivery of the married woman is done at her mother's house. After the child is born, the Pesh Imam or Bangi from a Masjid is called and he says two mantras into the ears of the child; Azaan into the right ear and Ikayat into the left. Then honey is applied to the tongue of the child and it is bestowed a name. Among the Muslims the child is considered as born, a Muslim. If a priest is not available, the ceremony is done at home by the elder in the house. Akika ceremony is performed on the 7th or 14th, 21st or 40th day after the birth, when a goat is slaughtered, one goat in the case of a girl and two in the event of a boy being born.

The second sacrament is Khatna intended for male children. It means the circumcision. It is called Sunta Korop in Konkani and the surgeon for this job used to come from outside Goa. But now most such operations are done in hospitals. A party is given thereafter to celebrate the event.

Bismilla is the third sacrament to initiate the child into education. There upon the child is taught the Quran etc. The fourth sacrament is Nikah or marriage.

The fifth sacrament is Vafat when phrases relating to God are read out to the dying person. After a person has breathed his last, his legs and arms are straightened out, eyes and mouth closed and he is laid down to rest with his head in the direction of Mecca. Before the body is taken to the Kabrastan (graveyard) he is bathed with a lot of soap and aromatic flowers, the ceremony being known as 'gusul' after which new clothes are worn on the body. He is laid in the kafan (coffin). Three outfits for men and five dresses for women are kept separately in the coffin. Some verses from the Quran are read out. The body is taken to the Mosque and kept there for sometime and people and priest say namaz prayers.

It is considered one's duty to take the dead body on one's shoulder. Women do not take part in the funeral procession. The coffin is then taken to the cemetery where close relatives lift up the coffin and bury it in the dug ground.

Later, three days of Ziyarat are observed at the house of the deceased, with recitations from the Quran. On the third day snacks, fruits etc are served to all who participated in the funeral procession. On the 9th day and the 40th day as well as after three months and six months, food is served to people on behalf of the deceased.

9

Art, Architecture, Fair and Festivals

ART AND CRAFTS OF GOA

A land of blended cultures, the unison finds expression in the art and crafts of Goa. While on a trip to Goa, its difficult to resist temptation to buy souvenirs. One can see temples and churches adorned with 'folk' paintings. These paintings usually depict scenes from Mahabharata or Ramayana or the new testaments. The museums and art galleries in Goa also carry numerous examples of the Goan art. And not just the churches and the art galleries, you can catch glimpses of how the Portuguese and Indian forms merge in humble house holds.

Among the crafts of Goa, there is no end. Its difficult to pick what is best, the exquisitely carved rosewood and teak furniture, the terracotta work or the 'visible everywhere' sea shells work. Even in today's Techno driven world, these hand made souvenirs look so inviting on the counters of shops.

The art and craft of Goa, like its culture has come out of a blend of Indo-Portuguese art forms. Capturing the fancy of Goans as well as tourists, Goa craft has won critical acclaim from the connoisseurs of the art world. Some prominent crafts forms in Goa are the bamboo craft, woodcarving, brass metals, sea shell crafts, paper mache and wooden lacquer ware.

Pottery And Terracotta

While pottery is art of traditional form made with earthen clay, terracotta is ceramic clay. These are the traditional crafts forms of Goa. Utility cum decorative items are made out of these such as flower garden pots, pen holders, ashtrays, bowls, statues of saints and goddesses. They also draw inspiration from religious or historical themes. Borde and Bicholim are two famous centres of earthenware, though pottery is made all over Goa.

Brass Metal Work

Brass items are very famous with tourists especially samais. This craft is available in plenty in the markets of Goa. Unlike utility items which are made from sheet metal, brass metal is a different thing. The craft is passed from one generation to another and practiced on heredity basis. Its used mainly for casting decorative items like oil lamps, church bells, candle stands, ashtrays and temple towers etc.

Laquerware / Wood turning

Wood turning is a form of woodcarving that is used to

create wooden objects (e.g. a bowl or a table leg) on a lathe using cutting tools. Wood turning differs from most other forms of woodworking, here the wood is moving while a (relatively) stationary tool is used to cut and shape it. You will get cradles, baby carts, toys, corner stands, etc in Goa made by wood turning.

Crochet And Embroidery

The importance of crochet in Goa can be realized by the fact that every bride brings her crochet and embroidery work as dowry which is then displayed to demonstrate her expertise in the craft. Crochet and embroidery in Goa is inherent to every household where it is passed from one generation to another. Though the craft of crochet and embroidery has been in India since time immemorial but it came to Goa with the arrival of nuns and missionaries in fifteenth century. And thus started this tradition of crochet and embroidery in Goa which has only improved in quality and design since. The items made are hankies, table clothes, children and ladies garments, pillow and cushion covers and bed spreads etc.

Bamboo Craft

Bamboo craft initially was more of a utility based thing where in 'mahras', a scheduled community made items required by farmers and fishermen. They made things to store food grains, sell fish. Many utility items made out of bamboo are still used in villages like baskets, valli and supli (for washing and cleaning rice) and dali used as floor cover or to dry food grains. With time this traditional craft has taken shape of decorative cum utility items. Different types of flower baskets, flower pots, letter stands, fans etc are some common items now sold.

Fiber Craft

Nuns from Kerela brought the fiber craft to Goa. Fiber articles were earlier produced for utility purposes. This craft comes in handy keeping in mind the changing living style. The function of fiber is combined with some ornamentation to bring out some attractive and colorful items. Shopping bags, ladies purses, coasters, wall hangings are made by some women organizations of Goa using banana or sisal fiber.

ARCHITECTURE IN GOA

Goa is a visual delight. Palm trees dotting the length of Goa make walking on its street a refreshing experience, while their houses and abodes give off an old world charm. Some of these residences are candy coloured and some have pastel hues, but they are all vibrant nonetheless.

Reminiscent of the Portuguese who colonised the state in 1510, the buildings in Goa are a reflection of the culture and aesthetics from Europe and also of the traditional Goan style of architecture.

Before the Portuguese arrived in Goa, the houses and other buildings were mostly made of mud (sometimes also laterite) and would have a thatched roof. Facing inwards towards a central courtyard, these houses had small windows devoid of any colour or design. Nevertheless, they were all rather thoughtfully constructed with a layer of mud, jaggery and lime, acting as a shield against the excessive heat during the summers and the sloppy roofs being a tool to drain away rainwater during heavy monsoons.

However, when the Portuguese arrived they brought with them their own style and techniques. Laterite was now being used more often and the constructions magnified the windows, with big windows replacing the smaller ones and the otherwise dull walls were now painted in a rainbow palette.

The structures all around Goa gradually became a reflection of its colonisers and continue to remain so even after they left the state in 1961.

"Corners of Goa can still be associated with Lisbon. In fact I noticed it the other way round too on my visit to Lisbon," says Rishad Saam Mehta, a travel writer from Mumbai.

Standing bright and beautiful, the houses around Goa speak for those who once inhabited them and the timeless beauty they left behind. The houses now roof Goans, whose ancestors, it is said, claimed them when they were abandoned by their previous owners.

While some walls have been re-done and look as good as new, some show intermittent modern influences.

PRINTING IN GOA

The art of printing first entered India through Goa. In a letter to St. Ignatius of Loyola, dated 30 April 1556, Father Gasper Caleza speaks of a ship carrying a printing press setting sail for Abyssinia from Portugal, with the purpose of helping missionary work in Abyssinia. Circumstances prevented this printing press from leaving India, and consequently, printing was initiated in the country.

The arrival of the first press

There is evidence that the use of the concept of mass duplication in India dates back to the time of the Indus Valley Civilization. Grants of land were originally recorded by engraving the information on copper plates and etchings on different surfaces like wood, bone, ivory and shells. However, printing arrived about a hundred years after the Gutenberg Bible was first printed.

Many factors contributed to the necessity of the initiation of printing in the subcontinent, the primary being evangelization and the Jesuits were solely responsible for this. Francis Xavier is known to have been teaching the *Bible* in Tharangambadi (Tranquebar), Tamil Nadu around 1542. Also, when the Viceroy of Goa, on behalf of King Joao III of Portugal, opened schools for Indians, Francis Xavier pressured Portugal to make printing presses available to India, Ethiopia and Japan. Meanwhile, the Emperor of Abyssinia (now Ethiopia) also requested Portugal to send a press along with missionaries. Consequently, the first batch of Jesuit missionaries, along with the printing press, left for Ethiopia on March 29, 1556, on a Spanish ship. The Patriarch designate of Abyssinia, Joao Nunes Barreto, as well as a team of technicians accompanied the press.

The prevalent route from Portugal to Abyssinia then required ships to round the Cape of Good Hope, touch Goa and reach Abyssinia. The press thus reached Goa, but soon after, news reached Goa that the Abyssinian Emperor was not keen on receiving the missionaries. Around the same time, the clergy in Goa felt the need for a printing press and on their request to the then Governor-General the press was made available to them. Thus, the press stayed in Goa. This was after Mexico had seen its first printing press, but preceded the press in Lima. The Patriarch designate Barreto was detained in Goa and it appears he never left India, but died in Goa on December 22, 1562.

Saint Paul's College and the first works printed

Printing operations began in Goa in 1556 (with the first printing press being established at the Jesuit Saint Paul's College in Old Goa), resulting in the publication of *Conclusiones Philosophicas*. 1557 saw the posthumous printing of St. Francis Xavier's *Catecismo da Doutrina Christa* five years after the death of its author. No extantcopy of this work is however, available.

Juan Bustamante and the early days of printing in India

The individual responsible for the initiation of printing in India was one Joao De Bustamante (rechristened Joao Rodrigues in 1563), a Spaniard who joined the Society of Jesus in 1556. Bustamante, who was an expert printer, along with his Indian assistant set up the new press and began to operate it. Among others, four books are known to have been printed by Bustamante:

- *Conclusões e outras coisas* (Theses and other things) in 1556.
- *Confecionarios* in 1557.
- *Doutrina Christa* by St. Francis Xavier in 1557.
- *Tratado contra os erros scismaticos dos Abexins* (A Tract against the Schismatic Errors of the Abyssinians) by Gonçalo Rodrigues in 1560.

The earliest, *surviving* printed book in India is the *Compendio Spiritual Da Vide Christaa* (Spiritual Compendium of the Christian life) of Gaspar Jorge de Leão Pereira, the Portuguese Archbishop of Goa. It was printed by Joao Quinquencio in 1561 and re-edited by Manuel de Araujo in 1600, and was embellished with ornate woodcut initials on each opening chapter. This was followed by the printing of Garcia da Orta's *Colóquios dos simples e drogas he cousas medicinais da Índia* on 10 April 1563 by Joao de Endem. In 1568, the first illustrated cover page (the illustration being done with the relief technique of woodblock) was printed in Goa for the book *Constituciones Do Arcebispado De Goa.*

Printing in the vernacular

Another Spaniard to play a major role in the history of printing in India was Joao Gonsalves, who is credited with preparing the first printing types of an Indian script- Tamil. However, since they were not satisfactory, new casts were made in Quilon(Kollam) by Father Joao da Faria. On 20 October

1578, these types were used to print the first book in an Indian language *in India* (the first Tamil book was printed in Lisbon in 1554 in Romanized Tamil script.)- Henrique Henriques's *Doctrina Christam en Lingua Malauar Tamul – Tampiran Vanakam*, a Tamil translation of St Francis Xavier's Doutrina Christa. This 16 page book of prayers and catechetical instructions was printed in Quilon. Though no extant copies of the first edition are available, MSS copies dating 1548-1614 are preserved in Lisbon and Rome. It should be mentioned here that Henriques was inducted into the Society of Jesus with the express intention of sending him to India to assist Francis Xavier. After the first press, a second press was set up. Not much is known about it save that it belonged to John Quinquencio and John Endem. The third press was set up in the St. Ignatius College, Rachol. Though Devanagari types were cast in 1577, the *Christa Purana* - an epic poem on the life of Jesus Christ written in the literary form of the Hindu *puranas* - was published not in Devanagari, but in the Roman script in the College of Rachol (1616 and 1649) and the College of St Paul (1654). This was primarily because of the clumsy shapes of the Devanagari types. In 1626, Diogo Reberio compiled the *Vocabulario da lingoa Canarim* (A Vocabulary of Konkani language) a Konkani-Portuguese and Portuguese-Konkani dictionary.

The 17th century saw the beginning of a large-scale book-printing in Goa, egged on massively by the need to print Christian texts for the benefit of the newly converted Christians. This time also saw a shift from the use of coercion to that of religious education for conversions. Thus, a number of books were printed in Konkani and Marathi due to the initiative of, among others, Father Thomas Stephens (who, in 1640, produced the first Konkani Grammar- the Arte de Lingua Canarin and in 1622, published *Doutrina Christam em lingoa Bramana Canarim, ordenada a maneira de dialogo, pera ensinar os mininos, por Thomas Estevao, Collegio de Rachol* or Christian Doctrines in the Canarese Brahmin Language, arranged in dialogue to teach children, which was the first book in Konkani and any Indian language), Father Antonio Saldanha, Father Etienne do la Croix, Father Miguel do Almeida and Father Diogo Ribeiro (whose *Declaraçam da Doutrina Christam*, or Exposition of Christian Doctrine in Konkani was printed in 1632). Despite the efforts of Father Stephens and the general familiarity of the Devanagari script, it was found easier to cast not Devanagari, but Roman types for Konkani. This was one of the major factors that alienated Konkani from other Indian languages, since the Roman script failed to fix a number of Konkani sounds that the Europeans faced difficulty in pronouncing. It was, however, this adoption of the Roman script for printing in the vernacular helped printing to flourish in Goa till 1684, when the official decree suppressed the vernacular languages and printing suffered a setback. Printing in Tamil stopped after 1612, and the last books printed in Latin and Portuguese before printing fairly died were published in 1674.

Ziegenbalg and the revival of printing

It was not till 1706 when Bartholomaeus Ziegenbalg, a Danish missionary, arrived at Tharangambadi that printing in India could flourish again. A printing press arrived around 1712-13 and the Tranquebar Press produced its first publications. On Ziegenbalg's insistence, the first Tamil publication from the press reached the mass in 1713, followed by the New Testament in 1714. It was as late as 1821 that printing was revived in Goa with the starting of a weekly called *Gazeta de Goa*, later known as the *Chronista Constitucional de Goa* (1835) and still later, the *Boletim de Governo do Estado da India* (1837).

Later years

From 1940 to 1960 there were four to six printers in Goa, of which the prominent ones were JD Fernandes, Gomantak Printers and Borkar Printers. Smaller entrepreneurs also joined the fray. One of these was a teacher in a local school in Churchorem. Rohidas Bandekar quit his profession to start a press—Bandekar Offset—with a meagre investment of Rs 24,000.

FOLK MUSIC AND DANCE

Mussoll

Mussoll is a folk-play-cum-dance played by the Kshatriyas among the Christians from the two hamlets of Chandor-Kott and Kouddi in Chandor village. Mussoll in Konkani, is an instrument used by women folk for pounding rice. It is a dance based on the legendry powers of the ancient Kshatriyas. This play must have been exhibited at the sabha-mandapa (assembly- hall) of the royal temple of Lord Chareshwar (moon god), with as many variations as circumstances of the time permitted. It is also called 'Musllam-Fell' or Khell. The dance is a war dance - a dance of a martial race or caste.

From the wording of the song, the Mussoll dance commemorates the victory of King Harihara II, son of Bukka I of the Vijayanagar empire, over the Cholas at the ancient fort of Chandrapur around 1310AD. King Harihara is supposed to have claimed descent from the lunar race. Mussoll dance has a constituent symbol, *i.e.* a bear which is the symbol of Cholas.

Originally the dance was held on the full moon night in the month of Phalguna. Now it is held on the second night of the Christian carnival. The preparation for the dance-cum-play commence on the first day of the carnival (*i.e.* Sunday). One of the most senior Gaunkars (Kshatriya or Chaddho) is eligible to become the captor of the bear. Dressed in ancient native costumes consisting of a Dhoti, over which he wears a white shirt like garment, a jacket and a turban and anklets on the left foot, he carries a rope in his hand and a ghumatt (which is a local percussion instrument in Goa consisting of goat-skin taut over the mouth of an earthen pot, of which the other mouth is kept open) slung down his neck.

Another Gaunkar dressed in a ragged black blanket, his face covered with a mask of a bear, a rope tied round his waist, the end of which is in the hands of the captor and carrying a branch of a mango or 'rumbodd' tree is taken prisoner by the captor, and exhibited to the Kshatriya households in the Kott area of Chandor.

Next day at six o'clock in the morning, both the captor and the captive bear proceed to the main gate of the Fort near San Tiagos Chapel (St. James). They come from the gate, the captor beating the ghumatt and the bear growling out, to the entrance of the chapel. There the captive bear, deposits the branch of the tree to signify total surrender. From there, they go along from house to house of the Gaunkars, care being taken to arrive last at the house of the captor where he and the captive bear change into their normal vestments and disband from there.

On the second day of the Carnival, at about 10 in the night, all Gaunkars assemble at the Sabha-mandapa of the temple of Lord Chandreshwar. A short Christian prayer is said and then the dance can begin at the Mandd which is a place, marked for communal festive functions.

When they have finished dancing, the procession led by torch bearers and attendants proceeds to the Chapel of San Tiago near the main gate of the Fort, where they dance for a while. Then they go from house to house of every Gaunkar and after the last house has been visited, they return to the 'Mandd' and disband. At every dwelling, the lady of the house must welcome the dancers by bringing out a lamp.

On the third day of the Carnival, at about ten in the morning, one Gaunkar dressed in the native costume and carrying a ghumatt and accompanied by a peasant woman who carries with her a basket of cow dung, a pot of water and a broom, takes the same route of the previous night, dance and sees that the barik rounnem (which is the central spot where the Mussoll was beaten hard into the ground during the dance) is levelled and cow dunged to signify the return of peace and to reassure prosperity and well being of the city inhabitants. A token coin is given to the sweeper-woman and another one to the Gaunkar as the households contribution to the Mandd fund. This fund serves to meet the incidental expenses of the dance performance and miscellaneous activities.

The Mussoll or pounding pestle used in the dance is made of solid bamboo of about 6-7 feet in length with inserted hawk's bells and is carried only by those who will actually dance. The torches are made of coconut, sliced mid-way longitudinally dried like copra and treated with a mixture of mud and cow dung. These were held upright on a spike at the end of a long bamboo stick. A wick was inserted, which burns under the oil that oozes out of the dried Kernel of the coconut. Besides these, torches of wax or of dried coconut-tree leaves will be used.

The dance consist of a march and the beating of the barik rounnem. The march has a martial beat and has three different steps. First a combination of clockwise and anti-clockwise full turns. Second a serpentine forward movement done in half turns, left and right and third as a straight march on the ball of the feet. The starting step is always with the left foot, except that in the first step whilst the left side dancers are completing the full turn starting with the left foot. The right dancers do the same starting with the right foot in order to keep the movement either clockwise or anti-clockwise.

The dance has only two beats: single beat and a triple time beat. The steps are basically a one-step and a three-step movement. But a combination of one-step, two step and three step movements each in clockwise and anti-clockwise turns is usually danced. The dance always starts with the left foot forward and in an anti-clockwise circular direction.

The most enchanting is the twirl in which every alternate dancer leaves the ring or the barik rounnem and they form together an outer ring dancing in an opposite direction in three-step movements, while the dancers in the inner circle barik-rounnem do the three-step movement in full turns. Though the original song of the Mussoll dance is on an eastern melody, it is weighed down by western music with the Portuguese impact on it.

Manddo

Manddo is a song or rather a poignant story of love told in the form of a lovely song. The word Manddo, derives from the Sanskrit 'mandalam' meaning circular movement. It is believed that originally the Konkani Manddo dance involved movement in circle. At present such circular patterns are noticed when the dancers get into a feverish pitch in the concluding stages of the dance. In the normal course the dance moves along parallel lines, with graceful movements to and fro, advancing and reading, the men displaying in a flourish towards the women their colourful handkerchiefs and the women admiring their toy fans, with an eye on the men.

The Manddo music appears to have been strongly influenced by Latin or rather Italian music. The dance-song Manddo may be called a synthesis of the Italian minuet and the temple Devadasi dance-song.

The singing moves majestically in a slow, andante rhythm, with dignity and grace. It falls into a drowsy dormant mood towards the fag-end of the singing function when the singers are tired and may have imbibed considerable quantities of alcohol and cannot go on much longer. The Manddo has attained the virtual status of a classical or art song after being subjected to a process of sophistication and stylisation. The ghumott provided the right beat, attuned as it is to Manddo singing and dance. The beat of it moves faster and faster as the singing progresses to a crescendo, on to a frenzy and conclusion.

Though the Manddo is a story of love told in song, there have been a few songs composed on a similar pattern but involving themes of a political nature called Political Manddo. There are Manddos on the revolts and uprisings of the Ranes, the legendary Warriors of the Sattari taluka of Goa, and the Christian Kustoba's feats of daring against the Portuguese government etc.

Every year a Manddo festival is held as an event of importance from 1966 onwards, with a special Bernardo Award for the best Manddo.

The Dulpod or Durpod

If the Manddo can be called an expression of the romantic aspect of the Goan, the Dulpod that follow it is the singing repertoire. The Durpod gives its couplets a compressed and catchy note providing fleeting glimpses of the variety of Goan life. It is a thing of joy and gaiety, evoking laughter, carefree in its mood and lively in its expression.

As the hunting melody of the Manddo moves towards a conclusion and ends, it is followed by the Dulpod, the beat of which is the opposite to that of the Manddo and more quick-moving, symbolising the lively sprightliness of life among the common folk. The Dulpod moves into a staccato beat and quickens in a syncopated rhythm.

The most popular among the Dulpods are the one about Cecila and her sewing, Modgonvam Thovyanger and 'Maya-ya-ya' or Lia-lia-lo. The Dulpod encompasses the whole of life in its infinite variety- human, animal and vegetables. All of it is captured in the Dulpod in couplets, whose effect in its wording, is very pithy and telling.

Deknni or Dakhnni

It is a form of song-cum-dance in the Christian repertoire of song among the people of Goa. It is a song composed by Christian artistes perhaps an expression of the Goan Christian nostalgia for their lost Hindu past, where the Devadasi or kolvont in Konkani was an alluring symbol.

The term Dakhnni in Sanskrit means devil of a female. It is danced in a manner that verges on the voluptuous, with gyrations and significant gestures which are so suggestive in character. The main danseuse is joined by other females, enticing in their appearance, who announce themselves to the audience.

Then begins the pleading and coaxing by the women, including finally the boatman with offerings of anklets, bracelets, nose-ringlets, by turns and finally clinching the deal with the offer of a kiss, which latter the boatman accepts in the surrender to their wiles, to ferry them across to the other side of the river to a place belonging to a man called Damu, where they have to perform at the wedding.

Kunnbi-geet

Kunnbi-geet is a folk song prevalent among the hardy labourers called Kunnbis which are sung to the accompaniment of the ghumatt and the drum and the clang of cymbals. These Kunnbis are found concentrated in the Chandor-Kouddi hamlet of Chandor in an exclusive ward of their own called Kunbeam-Vaddo now being called by them as Miream-Jirem. The theme of their songs varies from romantic love to bitter resentment and satire couched in suggestive language against their landlords (Bhakar) who have usurped their lands and are exploiting them. The Kunnbis sing songs at different times, like at different stages of cultivation of rice. It is done at the time of Nondnni (weeding), Mollnni (threshing), Luvnni (harvesting). Winnowing does not find expression in songs. There are also songs with reference to the rain and its bounty.

Occupational Songs among Workers

The Goan fisherman have their own folk-songs which they sing at the time of the Sangodd (two boats being tied together). The most famous of these performances being at Calangute, at the time of their first trips to the sea after the resumption of the fishing seasons after monsoons.

The toddy-tappers who are the largest group among the Sudir group of castes in Chandor, have their own charming songs called Rendrachim Geetam (songs of toddy tappers), which are equally fully of native verve. Other occupational songs are the Mitta-geet of salt pan workers and the Ghanno of the oil-mill crushers.

The general run of workers/labourers have another type of song sung at random at siesta time or may be during recreational hours, to the accompaniment of ghumatt and Kansallim (cymbals) which are known as tandnni which is derived from 'tan' (thirst). Such songs arise from the native soil have the freshness and smell of it.

Konkani songs of Goa are found in an infinite variety. For the song has been the mainstay of the Goan in his hour of joy and sorrow, even in the expressions of protest against injustice and oppression even when he was confronted with the threat of extermination.

The cradle songs in Goa are known as Painno or Halloio. Though they are very few in number, they are fine expressions of lilting tunes, the best of the existing ones being Painnem Halounk (to rock the cradle) and Dol re Baba (Rock, baby).

There are songs for various ceremonies connected with weddings. After the engagement is over, Goan Christians and Hindus follow more or less similar customs in their weddings. The songs that accompany the different stages and ceremonies of the wedding ritual are called Zoti.

Another lilting traditional song, sings of the cowherds and milkmaids who used to come down from the Ghats in search of plenty, in Goa and the regions around it. The song is sung alternately by choruses of two groups, boys and girls.

Talgoddi Dance

There are some activities which are peculiar to Goan Hindus. The spirit of the carnival finds its expression in Chandor village among the Hindus in the form of the Talgoddi dance. It literally means young men in rhythm in Konkani. It has eight distinct modes, expressed through its theme and is danced by eight to twelve men.

They show their skill in footwork and muscles by dancing a number of group dances, which are a spontaneous outburst of genuine folk spirit, on the Mandd or paved courtyard under the graceful and cool mattov (pavilion made of thatched green coconut, tree plaited leaves and mounted on betel nut poles). It is a sort of an aimless dance expressing a pure rhythmic pattern of human movements, energy and sheer joy of living.

Shigmo

Shigmo or Shimga is the Goan expression of the sprit of spring around the month of March, very close to the carnival. The focal hour of its celebration is the full moon day of the month of Phalguna. Shigmo is the time for the home coming of the brave, who had left their firesides with the Dussehra. For the farmer and the shepherd, it is the time of rebirth of nature and for the warriors, the time of return of man.

Ceremonial thanksgiving, processions to temples and shrines, songs, dramas and dances, bonfires, masquerades and abuses, festoons, banners, colours and sweets are in plenty on this occasion. Rang-panchami gets merged into the celebration with the throwing of colours in a boisterous manifestation of gaiety.

The other manifestations of Shigmo in Goa are the Romatt or Mell, Goff and Tonnya Mell, Dashavatari Khell and Kalo plays and dances. These are performed in most of the rural areas of Goa where Hindus predominate.

Foogddi

It is a dance very much loved among Goan Hindu girls and women. The details of the dance vary from caste to caste in Goa. Brahmin girls dance it with a brass pot on the head. Farmers, fisher folk and Kunnbis (Gavddis) dance it by forming an interlocked circle often of up to 12 girls. The Mahar women of Pednem area, dance it singly throughout, though in a group with exquisite footwork and attractive rhythm, which is kept up with foot claps every time the dancer revolves around herself.

At the Chovoth in Goa, nature revives the spirit of fulfilment with the season of fruitfulness. An uncontrollable explosion of energy sets the feet in motion. The girls and women start singing and dancing before Lord Ganesha. The most popular form of Foogddi in Goa is the one with circle formation which begins with the chanting of religious invocations. Konkani songs of special significance as well as of social themes follow upon the religious hymns. They are sung by first improvising some homely group activity like grinding, washing or kneading which provides them with a dramatic setting. In this conductive setting, the group exchanges opinions and information in crisp couplet and salacious stanzas. It can also include scandals and gossip about those who are absent from the scene.

After this first part in slow tempo, the group breaks up into pairs and with interlocked hands, swirls around with gradually increasing pace, singing songs of matching speed. When the swirling attains maximum speed, they simply keep up the rhythm by blowing air through the mouth, making Foo. -Foo sounds.

When totally exhausted after the song and dance they sink down with heady satisfaction, laughing yet looking jealously at the pairs still spinning like tops with the dizzy emissions of Foo..Foo..Foo.. in the air. This unique sound in the expression of the song has bestowed the name of Foogddi, on the dance form. Foogddi is an all weather indoor dance and needs no special religious occasion for performances. It is mostly danced on all important religious and social occasions. It may even form the tail-end portion of other dance forms like the "Dhalo".

Dhalo

This song-cum-dance is also an all women affair like the 'foogddi'. The language of the song is Konkani with a slight admixture of Marathi. Dhalo are played (khellttat) rather than danced (nachtat). They are played out on the moonlit winter nights in the courtyard of the house. They are slower in tempo, songs prevailing predominantly over the movements. The front yard of the house, where normally the newly harvested corn (paddy) is processed, is dug and paved carefully and later plastered with cow dung almost to a cement like finish. After the rice grains are winnowed, dried and stored, this paved place serves as a venue for all the socio-cultural activities of the village.

There is a specific spot close to the door step called a Mandd or station. Here every activity is initiated with a puja and a lamp lit. This spot is considered sacred and represents the spirit of the occasion. The courtyard is later covered with a canopy of woven coconut-tree leaves, supported by a framework of betel-nut-tree poles. This covering over the Mandd is called Mattov in konkani.

Participants start gathering in the courtyard by 9 PM on the moonlit night of the Pausha month, according to the Hindu calendar. As many as 24 women take part in each session of this dance-cum-song affair. They split up into two parallel rows of 12 each, facing each other and form a close-knit unit by linking themselves with arm-around the back arrangement, singing in unison. They sway, bend, move forward and backwards, singing songs of religious and social importance, unhappy and sad things of old, which are locally composed from memory and revised extempore with addition or change of words and lines here and there to suit the occasion.

The liveliest fun of a Dhalo session, occurs on the concluding day. The week which can be called women's lib week concludes with a sense of freedom. Therein women put on, all sorts of dresses of a fancy variety including those of various male roles, those of animals and birds and act out their respective parts and fantasies meticulously and with great dramatic gusto.

Ovi Songs

The Ovi songs relating to ceremonies of a profane nature like weddings etc are very much current in Goa among the Hindus, while they have almost disappeared among the Christians with few exceptions. They are sung by women while applying the coconut-pulp milk to the bride and groom, while preparing condiments for dinners etc. The most popular are those that concern with the spirit of fertility in the biblical terms of increase and multiply.

When the missionaries first began their work of spreading of Christianity in Goa, they made use of the existing Konkani metres, the main one used by them being the Ovi. People would gather around a fire or a cross and reverently sing Ovis composed by the missionaries in Konkani using biblical themes and other religious symbols.

Dantear Ovio meaning those ovis which are sung while grinding wheat and rice for various food preparations on the hand-mill (dantem in konkani) at wedding time, are sung in

Goa. As the women grind, they crush their worries and sorrows in a symbolical gesture. The best of these ovis are found in the villages of Savoi-Verem, Boma and Zambaulin.

ARCHITECTURE OF GOAN CATHOLICS

The Architecture of Goan Catholics has strong Portuguese, Mughal, and Indian influences. It developed over the long colonial Portuguese India era (1500s"1961).

Many of the 16th and 17th colonial Catholic churches were built in the Portuguese Baroque style. Most of the historic houses still standing were built between the 18th century and the early part of the 20th century, in a mix of Neoclassical and Gothic Revival styles.

Design influences

Factors that influenced residential design in Goa include:

- Protection from fierce seasonal monsoons.
- Portuguese Empire rule allowed Goan people to travel abroad; when they returned they brought with them ideas and influences from other countries. The Goan master builders executed these ideas using local building materials, making the Goan house a mixture and adaptation of design elements and influences from other cultures.
- The traditional Baroque architecture style of Portuguese-built churches.
- A European aesthetic/lifestyle was encouraged to separate newly converted Goan Catholics from their cultural roots. However, they adopted a European outlook but did not cut themselves off from their Indian roots completely, and resulting cultural fusion affected house design.

Exteriors

The traditional pre-Portuguese homes were inward-looking with small windows; this reflected the secluded role of women. The houses opened into courtyards, and rarely opened onto streets. The Catholic houses built or refurbished between the middle of the 18th and the 20th centuries were more outward-looking and ornamental, with *balcões* (covered porches) and verandas facing the street. The large *balcões* had built-in seating, open to the street, where men and women could sit together and 'see and be seen', chat with their neighbours, or just enjoy the evening breeze. These *balcões* are bordered by ornamental columns that sometimes continued along the steps and added to the stature of the house. This, together with the plinth, which usually indicated the status of the owners. The houses of rich landlords had high plinths with grand staircases leading to the front door or *balcão*.

Basilica of Bom Jesus, another example of Portuguese architecture

Large ornamental windows with stucco mouldings open onto verandas. These may appear purely decorative, but have their origins in similar mouldings in the windows of Portuguese houses. There these elements of style were devices to help sailors identify their homes at a distance as they sailed in. The design is therefore an import but serves a similar purpose in Goa: to help construct the identity of the home. Windows gradually became more decorative, ornate, and expressive.

Front doors were flanked by columns or pilasters.

Railings were the most intricate embellishment in a Goan house. Pillars, piers, and colours do not seem to be influenced by any style in particular; rather they conform to a rather mixed bag of architectural styles.

Cornices

Country tiles used as a corbel are a feature peculiar to Goa. The effect achieved is aesthetically pleasing, giving the roof projection a solid, moulded appearance.

Gateposts and Compound walls

Gateways consisted of elaborately carved compound walls on either side of the gate posts.

Use of colour

Dramatic and startling colour—initially achieved with vegetable and natural dyes—plays an important role in Goan architecture. Colour was decorative and used purely to create a sensation. With a colour wash, the house looked "dressed" and therefore displayed the economic well-being of the family that lived in it. Here art in architecture performed a social function. However, this was not completely a matter of individual choice, since during Portuguese rule the owner of the house could be fined if his house was not painted.

The walls were made of mud and then later of laterite stone; they were usually plastered then painted. Very few buildings are coloured exactly alike and solid colours are used for front facades; interiors are usually in paler colours/white with solid color highlights.

This rendering or piping in white is the result of the unwritten rule during the Portuguese occupation of Goa that no private house or building could be painted in white. Only churches and chapels enjoyed this privilege. It is understandable that Goan Christians followed this rule, as white was associated with the Virgin Mary and therefore the virtues of purity and chastity (both desirable in Goa), but, surprisingly, Goan Hindus also respected this practice. As a result of this code, an interesting and aesthetically pleasing trend developed, as competition among neighbours gave impetus to variety.

Interiors

Most houses are symmetrical with the entrance door occupying the place of honour. Typically this front door leads to a foyer which then either leads to the *sala* (the main hall for entertaining a large number of guests) or the *sala de visita* (a smaller hall for entertaining a small number of guests) and in some cases the chapel in the house. From here one can also directly enter the rest of the house, which usually revolved around a courtyard. Typically the master bedroom opens into the *sala* or is close to it. The dining room is usually perpendicular to these rooms; the bedrooms flank the courtyard, and the kitchens and service areas are at the rear of the house. In the case of two-story houses, a staircase, either from the foyer or the dining room, leads to more bedrooms.

Consisting of humble burnt earth plastered over with cow dung and hay, or with elaborate patterns made with tiles imported from Europe, the floors in Goan houses have been both workplaces and statements.

Almost all Goan houses have a false ceiling of wood.

Churches

The Portuguese regime, mandated the arrival of many Roman Catholic missionaries, particularly the Portuguese Jesuits, who were instrumental in building many churches in Goa. The Goan Catholic style of constructing churches thus came to be influenced by the Portuguese style. Notable are the Se Cathedral and Basilica of Bom Jesus.

FAIRS AND FESTIVALS IN GOA

There is a lot more than just the wonderful golden beaches lined up with swaying palm trees, the sparkling blue strip of ocean that runs parallel to the yellow sands and the colorful friendly people , that adds to the vibrancy called 'Goa'. The all year through joie de vivre of Goa, on the Western border of Indian subcontinent, is also attributed to the innumerable number of fairs and festivals in Goa, that gives the people here more reasons to celebrate.

In spite of being inhabited predominantly by the Christians, it is not only the Christian fairs and festivals, but also festivals of Hindu religion that are celebrated here with the same zeal and fervor. Other than the Hindu and Christian festivals and fairs in Goa, there are also people of other religions living in Goa, which creates a wonderful fusion of diverse cultures and traditions. It is through these fairs and festivals in Goa that one gets the idea about the wonderful underlying synthesis of all the different cultures and religions in Goa.

Goa Fairs And Festivals

People Celebrating Carnival in Goa

A group of people who are deeply religious and cultural despite being modern - that's how Goans are. The people of Goa are also an enthusiastic lot who love to live every moment of their life to the fullest. These two traits of Goans together make them extremely special. And when they are so special, can their fairs and festivals be in anyway ordinary? Of course not. The fairs and festivals of Goan are infact reflective of their very religious and cultural self. And as for the enthusiasm we mentioned earlier, you need to experience it to know what it actually is.

With a majority of Hindu and Christian population, the major festivals celebrated in the state definitely belong to these two religions. However, this does not imply that festivals of people following other religion are not celebrated in the state. Moreover, there are certain festival that are celebrated only in Goa. It is these festivals that make Goa so special. Varying in their themes, these festivals lend a unique charm to the state and attract tourists in large number.

FAMOUS GOA FESTIVAL

Goa Carnival

Feast of St Francis Xavier

The Feast of St Francis Xavier is held during the month of December, in the first week itself. The venue for the feast is the Basilica of Bom Jesus in Old Goa. St Francis Xavier is hugely renowned Christian saint and his feast attracts a whole lot of devotees from all over the country and even across the world. It is believed that even after his death, the body of the pious saint did not rot away like the rest of the mortals. Today, his body is preserved in a silver casket in the Bom Jesus and is displayed every ten years. After the last exposition in 1994, the authorities found out that the body is longer in a condition to be displayed, hence further exposition appears impossible in future. However, the feast is celebrated every year and if you wish to pay your respect to the saint, you can be a part of this feast.

Feast of Three Kings

This feast is celebrated in The Church Of Our Lady Of The Mount in Old Goa and is also known as the Festa Dos Reis or The Epiphany Day. The date for celebration is 6th of January. The special feature of this feast is that despite being a Christian festival, it is celebrated by Hindus with equal fervour. The Lady of Mount, as a mark of respect to whom this festival is celebrated, is believed to protect people and grant their wishes for children. The festival continues for nine days (ending at 6th Jan) and is marked by a lot of music and dance. On the last day three young boys dressed as kings reach the chapel after driving to different paths and offer the Lady of Mount everything they have. The rituals are followed by a fair where you can shop for a whole range of items ranging from meal to copper and brassware, furniture, clothes, toys, trinkets, sweetmeats, glass bangles and spices of all sorts.

Shigmotsav

This is yet another festival that is celebrated in the month of March from 11th moonday to 15th moonday. Shigmotsav is basically a festival of masses wherein people in different villages dress up beautifully and rejoice in the merrymaking of the festival. There is song on every lip as the group of people dance their ways to the temple. The highlight of the festival is the Rang Panchami during which people throw gulal (red colour) at each other.

Goa Heritage Festival

This festival is a combined effort of the Goa Heritage Action Group (an NGO based in Goa), the Corporation of the City of Panaji and the Department of Tourism, Government of Goa. The festival, now in its third year, aims to preserve and promote the built heritage of Goa. The festival is marked by performances from various artists as well as display of work of art by local artisans. The festival in short is not only meant to celebrate the cultural heritage of the state. Rather, it also makes an effort to inspire awareness and appreciation in the hearts of Goans with respect to their culture and the need to conserve it for the benefit of future generation.

Bonderam

The festival traces its origin during the Portuguese rule. Two villages on the Divar Islands, Piedalda and Sao Mathias, were constantly locked in conflict over property issues. The Portuguese stepped in and tried to resolve the issue. They introduced a manner of division of properties with flags of various nations. However, the villagers were in no mood to accept the changes and threw stones at the flags to knock them out. Today, on the 4th Saturday of August, the Bonderam festival remembers the same incident. Each section of the village has its own float and there is plenty of music to keep the entire atmosphere alive.

Sea Food Festival

As per its name, this annual Sea food festival celebrates the rich sea food of Goa. For five days at a stretch, reputed hotels and chefs hold a stall and offer wonderful sea food prepared by them. Not to be left behind, the housewives too make their contribution in turning this event into a joyful affair. The festival will be loved by all those who are fond of sea food in general and Goan sea food in particular.

Monte Music Festival

A pretty recent festival, started just few years back, the Monte Music Festival celebrates the coming together of western classical along with Indian classical form of music. The venue for the festival, which is organised by the combined efforts of Fundacao Oriente, Cidade de Goa and the Kala Academy, is Capela da Nossa Senhora do Monte (Chapel of Our Lady of the Mount). Performances are usually held for four days and provides a platform to a number of artists to display their talents in front of an appreciative audience.

Kesarbai Kerkar Music Festival

This annual festival, celebrated for the past 23 years, is a joy for the lovers of music and dance. The venue for the festival is the Kala Academy complex in Panaji and the time of the year is November.

Christmas and New Year Celebrations

When Festivals in Goa is talked about, Christmas is right at top in excitement and energy. In fact, there might not be another place in India, that celebrates Christmas and New year with such enthusiasm and gala. Throughout the week between Christmas and New year, Goa is drenched in the colors of festivities with numerous parties and cultural shows. The best place to enjoy the Christmas celebrations are the churches of Goa whereas beaches are the unparalleled destinations to go for new year extravaganza.

Hindu Festivals

Chovoth, Diwali, Gokulashtami, Holi, Lairai Jatra, Nagpanchami, Gudi Padwa, Raksha Bandhan, Ram Navmi, Vasco Saptah

Christian Festival

Christmas, Good Friday, Colva Fama, Margao Feast, Procession of Saints, Konsachem Fest, Sao Jaoa, Touxeachem Fest, Feast of St peter Paul.

Goan Festivals

Annual Mando festival, Fontainhas Festival of Arts

10

Education

The smallest state in India, Goa covers an area of 3,702 km. Situated on the western coast of India, Goa shares its northern boundary with Maharashtra. Karnatakacovers the eastern and southern boundary of the state. Panaji is the capital city of the state of Goa. One of the major tourist destinations in India, Goa also houses some of the best educational institutes of the nation. The education system here is comparatively better than many other states. According to the 2001 census report, the state has a literacy rate of 82%, well above the national average.

Goa University

Goa had India's earliest educational institutions built with European support. The Portuguese set up seminaries for religious education and parish schools for elementary education.

Founded circa 1542 by saint Francis Xavier, Saint Paul's College, Goa was a Jesuit school in Old Goa, which later became a college. St Paul's was once the main Jesuit institution in the whole of Asia. It housed the first printing press in India and published the first books in 1556. Medical education began in 1801 with the offering of regular medical courses at the Royal and Military Hospital in the old City of Goa. Built in 1842 as the Escola Médico-Cirúrgica de (Nova) Goa (Medical-Surgical School of Goa), Goa Medical College is one of Asia's oldest medical colleges and has one of the oldest medical libraries (since 1845). It houses the largest hospital in Goa and continues to provide medical training to this day.

Carmel College for Women is affiliated to Goa University. It was established more than 50 years to aid in closing the education gender gap.

Goa Medical College, previously called Escola Médico–Cirúrgica de Goa

According to the 2011 census, Goa has a literacy rate of 87%, with 90% of males and 84% of females being literate. Each taluka is made up of villages, each having a school run by the government. Private schools are preferred over government run schools. All schools come under the Goa Board of Secondary & Higher Secondary Education, whose syllabus is prescribed by the state education department. There are also a few schools that subscribe to the all-India ICSE syllabus or the NIOS syllabus. Most students in Goa complete their high school with English as the medium of instruction. Most primary schools, however, use Konkani and Marathi (in private, but government-aided schools). As is the case in most of India, enrolment for vernacular media has seen a fall in numbers in favour of English medium education. As per a report published in *The Times of India*, 84% of Goan primary schools run without an administrative head.

Some notable schools in Goa include Sharada Mandir School in Miramar, Loyola High School in Margao and The King's School in São José de Areal. After ten years of schooling, students join a Higher Secondary school, which offers courses in popular streams such as Science, Arts, Law and Commerce. A student may also opt for a course in vocational studies. Additionally, they may join three-year diploma courses. Two years of college is followed by a professional degree programme. Goa University, the sole university in Goa, is located in Taleigão and most Goan colleges are affiliated to it.

There are six engineering colleges in the state. Goa Engineering College and National Institute of Technology Goa are government funded colleges whereas the private engineering colleges include Don Bosco College of Engineering at Fatorda, Shree Rayeshwar Institute of Engineering and Information Technology at Shiroda, Agnel Institute of Technology and Design (AITD), Assagao, Bardez and Padre Conceicao College of Engineering at Verna. In 2004, BITS Pilani one of the premier institutes in India, inaugurated its second campus, the BITS Pilani Goa Campus, at Zuarinagar near Dabolim. The Indian Institute of Technology Goa (IIT Goa) began functioning from its temporary campus, located in Goa Engineering College since 2016. The site for permanent campus was finalized in Cotarli, Sanguem.

There are colleges offering pharmacy, architecture and dentistry along with numerous private colleges offering law, arts, commerce and science. There are also two National Oceanographic Science related centres: the National Centre for Antarctic and Ocean Research in Vasco da Gama and the National Institute of Oceanography in Dona Paula.

Goa Institute of Management located at Sanquelim, near Panaji is one of India's premier business schools.

In addition to the engineering colleges, there are government polytechnic institutions in Panaji, Bicholim and Curchorem, and aided institutions like Father Agnel Polytechnic in Verna and the Institute of Shipbuilding Technology in Vasco da Gama which impart technical and vocational training.

Other colleges in Goa include Shri Damodar College of Commerce and Economics, V.V.M's R.M. Salgaocar Higher Secondary School in Margao, G.V.M's S.N.J.A higher secondary school, Don Bosco College, D.M.'s College of Arts, Science and Commerce, St Xavier's College, Carmel College, The Parvatibai Chowgule College, Dhempe College, Damodar College, MES College, S. S. Samiti's Higher Secondary School of Science and Rosary College of Commerce & Arts.

GOA ENGINEERING COLLEGE

Goa Engineering College is located in Farmagudi, Ponda and is the oldest and foremost engineering college in Goa. Founded in 1967, it is a government run college also known as Government Engineering College, Goa College of Engineering, Goa. It is the only NBA accredited degree level engineering college in the state of Goa.

Current Branches: The college presently has six branches of engineering, namely, Civil, Mechanical, Electrical & Electronics, Electronics and Telecommunication, Computer Engineering and Information Technology. Courses in Mechanical, Civil and Electrical were started since inception.

Further courses were then added: Electronics and Telecommunication in 1982, Computer Science in 1988 and Information Technology in 2001.

The National Board of Accreditation (NBA) has accredited 3 branches of the college. (Mar-Apr '06) They are the Mechanical, Civil and Electronics and Telecommunications branches of the College. This means the academic curriculum and the teaching learning process is of a good standard, with adequate infrastructure and faculty, acceptable to the All India Council of Technical Education (AICTE) the autonomous body, created by a bill in Parliament which overlooks at maintaining standards in technical education in the country.

Engicos

The students of Goa Engineering College call themselves *Engicos*. The college hosts their cultural festival, "Happenings", once every year, which features Goa's premier rock show and has hosted bands like Zero, Millennium in 1997, Parikrama in 1998, Pentagram in 1996 and 1999, Ezee Meat in 1997, Brahma in 2000, PDV, Moksha, Metakix, Psychomotor, Sceptre in 04-05.

The college also has one of the foremost installations of the E-learning software hosted by the Mechanical Engineering Department. It is a Free and Open Source Software and is called MOODLE (Modular Object Oriented Dynamic Learning Environment).

The college has a very active Nature Club which organises occasional tree planting programmes in the Farmagudi campus and organises treks to many exciting trekking locations in Goa. Some of the treks conducted were to Dudh Sagar, Keri, Mainapi falls, Tamdi Surla falls. etc.

Current Intake: The college has an annual intake of almost 360 students in different branches. This was increased from the existing 150 in 2001. The college continues to foster brilliant, competent engineers despite the dilution of talent due to the commencement of two more private engineering colleges in the state and the increase in intake.

Prominent Alumni: Among the prominent alumni of the GEC is Ashank Desai (Class of 1971), who currently heads the prestigious Mumbai-based Indian software firm called Mastek. The other famous alumnus is Prof. Mangesh Korgaonkar of IIT Bombay.

Prestigious Events

Happenings: An All-Goa Youth Fest organised by Goa Engineering College.

Richard M Stallman founder of the GNU Project and the Free Software Foundation visited the Goa Engineering College, and delivered a talk in November 2002.

BIRLA INSTITUTE OF TECHNOLOGY AND SCIENCE

Birla Institute of Technology and Science, Pilani, Rajasthan, India (popularly known as 'BITS Pilani') is one of the oldest and leading technology schools (along with IITs) of India. In addition to Pilani, BITS has campuses in Dubai, United Arab Emirates and Goa, India, an extension centre in Bangalore, India, and a fourth campus under construction in Hyderabad. The institute is privately supported, fully residential, and admits both male and female students.

Brief History: It was founded by Shri Ghanshyam Das Birla in 1929 as an intermediate college.

During World War II, the Government of India established a technical training centre at Pilani for the supply of technicians for defense services and industry. At the end of the war, in 1946, it was converted it into the Birla Engineering College with degree programmes in electrical and mechanical engineering.

In 1964, the Birla Colleges of Arts, Commerce, Engineering, Pharmacy and Science were merged to form the Birla Institute of Technology and Science (BITS). In this period of inception (especially during 1964-1970), BITS Pilani received support from the Ford Foundation and benefited from an alliance with the MIT.

BITS Pilani started to expand in India and abroad since 2000. New campuses were established in Dubai, United Arab Emirates (2000) and Goa, India (2004), and a fourth campus is to be opened in 2007 at Jawaharnagar (near Hakimpet Air Force station), Hyderabad. BITS also runs a virtual university and an extension centre in Bangalore.

Reputation and Rankings: Many reputed sources, including the *UNESCO Science Report 2005* make use of *Asiaweek* magazine's latest rankings of science and technology schools in the Asia-Pacific region, 2000. According to this ranking, BITS Pilani was ranked in the Top 20 in Asia (overall), and in the Top 5 in Asia in terms of 'Student Selectivity'.

The management programmes offered by BITS Pilani have also been ranked by *Asiaweek* (Top 30 Best Full-Time MBA, Top 30 By Reputation, Top 5 Distance MBA). These programmes have also been profiled by *Business Week* Online (The Best B Schools). Recently BITS-Pilani has upgraded its reputed 4 year MMS first degree to a 2 year MBA programme to meet the industrial demands.

Annual rankings of engineering colleges in India have been published by the magazine *India Today* since 1997. BITS Pilani was ranked in the Top 5 consistently (1997-2004) and ranked higher than a few IITs, but opted out of the survey since 2005. However, the institute participates in the *Dataquest*-IDC Survey as well as in the *Outlook*-Cfore Survey, and was ranked in the Top 5 T-Schools of India 2006 by both these surveys.

"BITS Pilani" was also the only Indian university to be ranked in the Top 20 Wired organisations of Asia by *Business Today* (January 18, 2004 issue).

The institute is accredited (with a five-star rating) by the Government of India's *National Assessment and Accreditation Council* (NAAC) for the period ending February 7, 2007.

BITS Pilani is also the institute of choice for toppers of the school leaving examinations in India. For instance, toppers of 21 educational boards including the CBSE and the ICSE chose to join the Institute in 2006. BITS Pilani is also reputed for an array of work integrated learning programmes for HRD of a vast spectrum of Indian corporates.

The Institute has strong alliances with various Indian/foreign universities/industries for exchange of students/faculty, Distance Learning Programmes, etc. A small list of colleges is given below:

1. MIT, Boston,
2. University of Maryland,
3. University of Otago,
4. University of Southern California,
5. Kathmandu university
6. University of Oklahoma,
7. Victoria University,
8. Kansas State University,
9. Arizona State University,
10. University of New South Wales,
11. Purdue University, and many more.

Undergraduate Admission Procedure: BITS admits students through revised admission procedure since 2005 via National Entrance Examination (BITSAT). BITSAT is Testv conducted online held between May 1 and June 10 in many cities all over India. The exam tests subject-content in English, Physics, Chemistry, Mathematics and Logical reasoning, and is focused on higher secondary curriculum in India. Prospective students are required to obtain minimum 80% marks in Physics, Chemistry and Mathematics in their higher secondary examinations to be eligible for admission.

Toppers of higher secondary examinations are exempted from taking BITSAT test and are considered admitted. This exemption helps ensure that BITS retain the significant number (about 20) of first rank holders from across the country who join BITS every year.

Acceptance rate in BITS is very low (Selectivty -> 2.6% in 2006) making it one the toughest schools in India and the world to get admission into.

Masters in Business Administration: Recently BITS-Pilani has upgraded its reputed 4 year MMS first degree to a 2 year MBA programme to meet the industrial demands. The programme is offered in the field of IT enables services and Engineering Technology, which by itself stands out of all other MBA degree. BITS offers these specialization owing to the strong need of technical knowledge for modern managers. A group of highly qualified core faculty, visiting faculty and practitioners imbue the students with contemporary knowledge base, business analysis and information based decision making skills thus spawning illustrious corporate executives, entrepreneurs and academicians world-over in its existence of over three decades. Selection is after an All India Entrance Test comprising of Technical Tests, an Aptitude Test, Group Discussions and a Personal Interview. The characteristic features of this programme includes:

Campus

Highlights

- Located on the banks of Zuari river, about 5 km from the airport.
- Spread over 188 acres of land owned by the Zuari industries.
- Newly constructed hostels for students.
- An air conditioned auditorium with seating capacity of 2200.
- Air-conditioned classrooms and lecture halls.
- An excellent library.
- Student activity centre.
- Shopping complex including a cafeteria.

Hostels: Well furnished hostels with single room accommodation is provided to all the students. Presently, there are 11 hostels, 8 hostels for boys and 3 hostels for girls, all with a 100mbps LAN connection in every room. Few more hostels are also being built for the next coming batch. Apart from this all the hostels are well connected to the main building through ingeniously designed walkways that protect the students from rain and the sun, with the exception of BH6, BH7 and BH8. Also every hostel has a common room with a tv and a phone with intercom facility.

Latest News

- BITS 360° - BITS Goa Virtual Campus Tour.
- Scream 2006 successfully completed on.
- The campus successfully organized an International Workshop On Biosensors (February 21-23 2006)
- Formally inaugurated on 5 may, 2006 by the honourable prime minister of India, Dr. Manmohan Singh.
- CSD (Centre for Software Development) launched an unofficial student forum.
- Abhigyaan-Literacy Mission to teach the underprivileged was started under the able guidance of Dr. T.C. Goel, the Director of Goa campus.
- PS1 (Practice School-1) which is on the lines of Pilani Campus was successfully completed for the 1st batch of students. Over 200 reputed companies participated in the process.
- The 3rd batch of the new campus joined on 1 august, 2006.

Annual Festivals

APOGEE: A Professions Oriented Gathering Over Educational Experience (APOGEE)—it is the annual Technical Festival of BITS, Pilani with projects ranging from Generational Garbage Collector for Highway Traffic Control Systems to Natural language Parsers to Optical Character Recognition Tools. The highlights of this 5 day festival are the many projects on display by the students, technical paper presentations, numerous contests (both fun science and hard-core tech), Cyberfiesta (software design contest) and the two quizzes: Brain of BITS (BOB), which have teams of one, and Over Head Transmission (OHT), a team quiz. Also, the Computer Science Association conducts an event called Gamophilic for all the gaming freaks, wherein famous multiplayer games like Quake and Counter Strike are organised.

BOSM: The BITS Open Sports Meet (BOSM) is the annual All India sports festival held in the month of September organised entirely by the students of BITS, Pilani. It attracts as many as 1000 participants from all over India.

OASIS: Oasis is an All India cultural festival organised entirely by the students of BITS, Pilani. Oasis is organised in the month of October. Around 1200 Participants from colleges all over India participate in Oasis.

The Budget of the fest is around 26 lakhs (*i.e.*, Rs 2.6 million). For the past 35 years, Oasis has been providing a platform to students from all over the country to showcase their talent and is a highly coveted event.

For BITSians, OASIS is a passionate exercise for perfection to make something in an inward condition of the mind and spirit rather than having something in an outward set of circumstances.

For BITSians OASIS is the widening of the mind and of the spirit and epitomizes the process by which a person becomes all that they were created capable of being.

For BITSians OASIS with a budget of 26 Lakhs is all about Passion driven by Passion and that is why it continues to remain as the jewel in the crown among college festivals in India name it Pulse, Mood Indigo, Spring Fest, Saarang, Antaragni, Alcheringa, Rendezvous, Thomso and what not.

October each year is the time of metamorphosis of BITS-Pilani. The quaint town in the middle of a desert turns into a pulsating amalgam of youth. A dollop of dance, a sprinkle of drama, a dash of quizzing with a delectable garnish of music sets up a recipe of fun for nonstop 96 hours that none would like to miss.

For a BITSian, every OASIS is a passionate Project which is non routine, non repetitive, one time undertaking, with time, cost and performance goals. If you have doubts about this, ask any of our headline hogging BITS Alums i-flex Rajesh Hukku, Texas Pacific Vivek Paul, ATA Airlines Subodh Karnik, Cisco Amit Sinha Roy, Reflexis Palakurthi, Bharat Forge Baba Kalyani, PMO office MOS Prithivi Raj Chauhan, Harvard Professor SP Kothari, Film Maker Mani Shankar, Music Maker Vivek Philip, Film Star Anu Hassan, Fiction writer for Penguin Shashi Warrier, Picador award winner for nonfiction Dilip D'Souza, Bridle Ramki and a galaxy of others shining in every profession one can think of to vouch for it.

OASIS indeed is a once in a lifetime experience that no one even remotely connected with it once, would even dream of missing ever again.

SANGAMAM: The annual classical music and dance festival conducted by Ragamalika. It is a three day cultural festival held in the last weekend of February. It features eminent artistes from all over the country performing for a cosmopolitan audience of over 2000. Sangamam also features a scintillating inaugural performance by the hosts before the artistes take their bow on the centre stage. Being personally involved in all stages of its planning, organization, finances and sponsorship, Sangamam is an event that every member of Ragamalika looks forward to and is widely popular among the BITSian fraternity.

Scheduled from 23rd to 25th February 2007, this year's Sangamam featured Carnatic Muisc Maestro Dr. T. V. Sankaranarayanan on the first day, Sitar- Flute Jugalbandhi by Shri Ravi Kiran and Shri Pravin Godkhindi on the second day and Ballet by Smt. Ananda Shankar and Group on the last day.

While on Day 1, Maestro Sankaranarayanan's voice drowned BITSians in an ocean of mixed emotions, the second day lifted them to level with the haunting Flute Sitar jugalbandhi and the third day Kuchipudi and Bharathanatyam carried them floating in the sky.

Sangamam 2007 indeed has surpassed the previous ten years in terms of brilliance and grandeur.

Conquest-The International Business Challenge

The Centre for Entrepreneurial Leadership (CEL) has been set up "to create business leaders in all spheres of life with an entrepreneurial thinking." Conquest (Conquest - The Business Challenge) is a unique business event conducted by CEL which helps to transform ideas into reality. This business-plan competition includes intensive mentoring by industry champions and a rigorous simulation involving real-life start up conditions.

The Winners share a prize money of INR 2 lakh and they are offered free incubation in the Technology Business Incubator at BITS Pilani. They are also given an opportunity to pitch their business ideas to some of the best VC forums in the country.

Interface: Interface is an event linking Engineering, Science and Management disciplines so characteristic of the broad based educational system of BITS Pilani Rajasthan India. Interface, the annual All India Management convention organized by the Management Association of BITS, Pilani encompasses a wide spectrum of activities. During the three days through which the convention spans, the organizing and the innovative skills of the students are tapped to the maximum.

The Management curriculum at BITS Pilani emphasizes on the theory and practice of Technology, Innovation and Engineering Management with focus on planning, development and implementation of technological capabilities to shape and accomplish the strategic and operational objectives of any organization.

BITS Pilani campus has over 4000 students who have varied interests and hail from different parts of the country. In addition, girls constitute roughly 40% of the total enrolment. The girls enrolment for the management curriculum alone at BITS Pilani was an astonishing 67.50% in the year 2004 which must be shocking to MS Julia Tyler, Associate Dean for the London

Business School MBA programme who has been wondering why the number of women studying MBA worldwide flatlined at about 27 percent. The enrolment of girls for the Management curriculum at BITS Pilani is one factor which none of the 100 B Schools in the latest Financial Times Global MBA Rankings 2006 can match.

The dynamic and versatile nature of the 4000 students at Pilani represents the most aggressive consumer age group of 18-25 years. Further, the high percentage of girls enrolled here with educational empowerment are powerful agents of social change. Interface is one occasion at BITS Pilani when publicity can flex its arms to the maximum and derive maximum mileage.

Over the past 27 years, Interface has metamorphosed into one of India's foremost management conventions. Management students and professionals from all corners of the country meet for a three-day showdown, to exchange ideas and to update themselves on the latest developments in the world of management. To this is added a splash of entertainment in the form of Management games, Business quiz and Workshops, conducted on an all India basis.

WAVES: The BITS-Pilani, Goa Campus annual culfest cultural festival. It is organized entirely by the students of BITS-Pilani, Goa Campus. It is the only institute in the country where the event was taken to inter-collegiate level within 1 year of its inception.

ZEPHYR: BITS-Pilani, Goa campus annual interhostel festival. It is organized by the students association in BITS-Pilani, Goa campus and invokes strong inter hostel rivalry. There are a total of 12 hostels with the numbers expected to increase next year. Zephyr 06 was just completed with Bh-2 emerging winners followed closely by Bh-1.Bh-8 finished third.

INSTITUTE OF MANAGEMENT

The Goa Institute of Management (GIM) is a business school located in the state of Goa, India.

The autonomous school is governed by a Board, and offers

a full-time MBA (PGDBM) programme (2 years) and executive MBA (3 years) and also is a resource centre for PhD programmes in Management for Goa University. Current MBA classes have a size of approximately 120 students. Present Director of Goa Institute of Management is Prof. Ranjan Ghosh.

History: Located on the banks of the beautiful Mandovi river in Goa, the Business School was founded in 1993 when Fr. Romuald D'souza (ex Director-XLRI (Xavier Labour Relations Institute), Jamshedpur and XIMB (Xavier Institute of Management, Bhubaneswar) moved from XIM, Bhubaneswar to create a centre of learning and excellence in Goa.

Infrastructure: The Campus, located at Ribandar, on a hillslope, is housed in a Heritage Building Santa Casa De Misericordia The Royal Portuguese Hospital, dating back to the Portuguese Rule in Goa.

The building, in which the school is housed, is supposed to be one of the earliest Hospitals in India and only in 1993 was converted from a Hospital building to a Business School Campus.

Keeping its Hospital legacy, some of the campus blocks still carry their past names. The various blocks are

- Admin
- Library
- Office
- Operations Theatre known as OT
- Morgue
- Hill Top
- Ladies Hostel
- Joe's
- The Quadrangle (Quad)
- Mess
- Jaggu's
- Kailash

Library: The library subscribes to most major national and international business and industry publications. The Institute provides access to various online databases and sources of information like Proquest, CMIE, Capitaline, and EBSCO.

Affiliations and Linkages

- Approved by the All India Council of Technical Education of the Government of India (AICTE) for offering postgraduate courses in management at the MBA level.
- Recognized by the Government of Goa and by many of the major industrial corporations in the country
- Member of the International Association of Jesuit Business Schools, which facilitates linkages for collaboration and exchange among some 60 Business Schools in 25 different countries in various parts of the world.
- Hosted Joint Study projects for two years in which 12 MBA students of Ohio University in Athens, Ohio, USA, under the guidance of their faculty, have worked with 12 GIM students in teams of four, on projects assigned to them by local industries.
- Ongoing tie-up with The University of Antwerp (Universiteit Antwerpen) for facilitating student interaction and joint study.
- Student exchange programme with, Fachhochshule Ingolstadt, Germany (up to 5 students).

Ranking

- Indian Business Magazine BusinessWorld India has ranked GIM as 18th in Best B-Schools in India for the year 2004.
- August 23, 2005, GIM ranks amongst the 15 Top institutes offering the MBA degree or equivalents in India
- GIM has been ranked 17th in the Business World India's Cosmode BW survey for the year 2005.

Upcoming Events

Past Events

- Conferencia Logistica, on 2nd and 3rd September'06- A Nationwide Logistics conference
- Patent Symposium 2005
- Confabulations 05

Alumni

- Mrunmay Das-Chief Investment Officer, Azim Premji Investments (P) Ltd.
- Gagan Banga, Executive Director, India Bulls
- Vishal Jain, Fund Manager, Benchmark MF
- Abhishek Agarwal,Managing Director, Relq International Ltd, Mauritius
- Perry Goes-Assistant VP, United Breweries
- Abhishek Jha, EA to CEO, Bajaj Hindusthan
- Ketan Hajarnavis, COO, Calibre
- Sridhar V.,CFO, RAK Investment Authority, UAE
- Maneesh Dangi, Fund manager- Birla sunlife mf
- Mohammad Qureshi, Director, Duracell
- Dwijendra Srivastava, Fund manager-JM Financial Asset Management Pvt. Ltd.

UNIVERSITY

Goa University,the seat of higher learning in Goa was set up in 1985 and merged with the existing Centre for Post Graduate Instruction and Research (CPIR) of the University of Bombay (now Mumbai) that functioned at state-capital Panaji or Panjim. Goa University offers both graduate and post-graduate studies and research programmes. It is currently (September 2006) accredited to the NAAC (National Assessment and Accreditation Council) in India with a rating of four stars. It is located on the Taleigao Plateau. Goa University was established under the Goa University Act of 1984 and commenced operations on June 1, 1985. The University provides higher education in the Indian state of Goa.

Centre for Education: Goa University is considered the centre for higher education in Goa, a former Portuguese colony and now India's smallest state, which has only a single university for its population of 1.4 million people.

Gujaral-designed: Goa University was designed by painter, sculptor, muralist, graphic designer and architect Satish Gujral. However, there has been some criticism of the type of model he envisioned for Goa University, considering that the coastal state receives a high amount of rainfall ever year and his structure might have not been the most suited from the climatic point of view.

Location: Goa University is built on a plateau called the Taleigao Plateau, located around five kilometres from the Goan state capital of Panaji or Panjim. It can be approached either via Bambolim to Dona Paula-Taleigao.

The Taleigao plateau overlooks the beautiful Arabian Sea and the picturesque Dona Paula shores, a former beach village now a tourist location. The University is also counted as one of the must-sees by many tourist guides, who route visiting tourists around this region.

Mandate: Goa University says its tasks are:

- Providing higher education under various faculties to the State of Goa.
- Providing facilities for research in various fields.
- Providing degrees in various faculties to all the successful candidates.

Bachelor's Degrees: The University is responsible for the bachelors' level of education conducted by different colleges across Goa, and affiliated to Goa University.

The following are the non-professional colleges affiliated to Goa University:

- The Parvatibai Chowgule College, Margao, Goa.

- Shree Damodar college of commerce and Economics, Margao, Goa.
- Carmel College of Arts, Science & Commerce, Nuvem, Salcete, Goa.
- Rosary College of Commerce & Arts, Navelim, Salcete, Goa.
- St. Xavier's College of Arts & Science, Mapusa, Bardez, Goa.
- M.E.S. College of arts and commerce, Zuarinagar, Goa.
- DM's College of Arts, S. P.Vaidya College of Science & V.N.S.Bandekar College of Commerce, Mapusa, Goa.
- P. E. S. College of Arts & Science, Farmagudi, Goa.
- Dhempe College of Arts & Science, Panjim, Goa.
- G.V.M.'s Shri Gopal Govind Poi Raiturkar College of Commerce & Economics, Farmagudi, Ponda, Goa.
- C. E. S. College of Arts & Commerce, Cuncolim, Goa.
- The Naval Academy, INS Mandovi. Veer, Goa.
- Government College of Arts, Science & Commerce, Sanquelim, Goa.
- Government College of Arts, Science & Commerce, Khandola, Goa.
- Government College of Arts, Science & Commerce, Quepem, Goa.
- Saraswat Vidyalaya's College of Commerce & Management Studies, Telangnagar, Khorlim, Mapusa, Goa.
- X. E. S. Fr. Agnel College of Arts & Comm, Pilar, Goa.
- Government College of Arts & Commerce, Pernem, Goa.
- Shree Mallikarjun College of Arts & Commerce, Delem, Canacona, Goa.
- Zantye Brothers' Educational Foundation's Narayan Zantye College of Commerce Sarvan, Bicholim, Goa.

- Goa College of Home Science,D. Bandodkar Road, Campal,Panjim, Goa.
- Goa Dental College and Hospital, Bambolim, Goa.
- Goa College of Architecture, Campal, Panaji, Goa.
- Institute of Nursing Education, Old I.P.H.B. Complex, Altinho, Panaji, Goa.
- Devi Shreevani Education Society's Goa Institute of Management Studies,M. S. College of Law Bldg.P. O. Caranzalem, Panjim, Goa.
- V. V. Mandal's Institute of Management Training and Research, Govind R. Kare Road, Margao, Goa.
- National Hydrographic School,Vasco da Gama, Goa.
- I N S Hamla,Marve, Malad(W), Mumbai - affiliated to Goa University.
- S. S. Dempo College of Commerce & Economics, Altinho, Panjim, Goa.

The following are the professional colleges affiliated to Goa University:

- V. M. Salgaocar College of Law, Miramar, Panjim, Goa.
- G. R. Kare College of Law, Margao, Goa.
- G. V. M.'s College of Education, Ponda, Goa.
- B. S. P. Gomantak Ayuveda Mahavidyalaya, Vajem, Ponda Road, Shiroda, Goa.
- Goa Salesian Society, Don Bosco College, Panaji, Goa.
- Nirmala Institute of Education, Altinho, Panaji, Goa.
- Shree Rayeshwar Institute of Engineering & Information Technology, Shiroda Goa.
- Goa Medical College, Bambolim, Goa.
- Goa College of Pharmacy, Panjim, Goa.
- Goa College of Music, Altinho, Panaji, Goa.
- Institute of Psychiatry and Human Behaviour, Bambolim, Goa.
- PES College of Education, Farmagudi, Ponda, Goa.
- College of Engineering, Farmagudi, Ponda, Goa.

Post-graduate Departments, Centres of Studies

On campus, Goa University has 23 post-graduate departments and two centres of studies offering academic programmes which lead to the Masters and Doctorate (Ph.D) programmes across different disciplines. Similarly, the university also conducts post-graduate diploma programmes in select disciplines.

The university houses 12 faculties, under which different departments operate and offer masters or diploma programmes. The following are the faculties in Goa University and the different departments which operate under them.

These include:

- *The Faculty of Language and Literature:* The Departments of English, Hindi, Konkani, Marathi, French and Portuguese.
- *The Faculty of Natural Sciences:* The Departments of Chemistry, Computer Science and technology, Earth Science, Physics (Electronics), Physics and Mathematics.
- *The Faculty of Social Sciences:* The Departments of Economics, History, Political Science, Philosophy and Sociology.
- *The Faculty of Life Sciences and Environment:* The Departments of Botany, Bio-technlogy, Micro-biology, Marine science and Zoology.
- *The Faculty of Commerce:* The Department of Commerce.
- *The Faculty of Management Studies:* The Department of Management Studies.
- The Faculty of Medicine.
- The Faculty of Engineering.
- The Faculty of Law.
- The Faculty of Performing, Fine Arts and Music.
- The Faculty of Design.

Centres: The University also houses two centers,

- The Centre of Latin American Studies.
- The Centre of Women's Studies.

New Courses: The master's programme in biotechnology is supported by the Department of Biotechnology (DBT) of the Government of India. Degree programmes in Physical Education and Fire Technology have been added during the academic year 2004-05.

Four year B.Sc (Nursing) degree has been added during the academic year 2005-06. In addition, the Goa University has also launched a Portuguese language course through its distance-education DEITE in 2005-06. Goa University's M.Com (Distance Education Mode) degree was launched in 2005-06.

Facts and Figures

- Goa University is located on the outskirts of Panaji or Panjim, and is spread over nearly 173 hectares on the Taleigao Plateau, overlooking the scenic Zuari River, adjoining the Arabian Sea.
- It also offers courses in Latin American Studies, and is one of the few universities in India to do so.
- Goa University claims to have one of the "best teacher-student ratios". But it has also been criticised in the past for having a limited number of students.
- It has established a remote sensing laboratory, with financial and technical assistance from the Indian Space Research Organisation.
- The university is situated in the Western Ghats region, which is known to be rich in flora and fauna.
- Goa University also has set up a unit for fungus-culture collection and research.
- Goa University has signed memoranda of understanding with a number of institutions, including the National Institute of Oceanography, Goa, Indira Gandhi National Open University, New Delhi, Universidade Moderna and University of Aveiro in Portugal, National Centre for Software Technology, Mumbai, International Rice Research Institute, Philippines, Atomic Research Centre, Mumbai, among others.

- Goa University offers a course on online programme in GIS, in association with the Centre for Geoinformatics, University of Salzburg, Austria.

Recognised Institutions: Recognised institutions functioning with Goa University recognition are:

- National Centre for Antarctic & Ocean Research, Vasco
- Directorate of Archives, Panaji
- National Institute of Oceanography, Dona Paula
- Xavier Centre for Historical Research, Porvorim
- Malaria Research Centre, Panaji
- Thomas Stephens Konknni Kendr, Porvorim
- Fishery Survey of India, Mormugao
- All India Institute of Local Self Government, Panaji

Admission Procedures

- The procedure for above is mentioned in detail in the annual handbookpublished and made available during the first week of June, each year.
- More information on admission can also be directly obtained from the academic sections, concerned departments, or colleges in person.
- All the admission forms are directly received by the concerned office of the various departments on the University campus.
- Members of the public can visit the office from 12.00 noon to 13.00 hrs. on all working days, according to the Citizen's Charter of the Goa University.

University Team: As of September 2006, the Governor of Goa S.C. Jamir is the chancellor of the university, with Prof P.S. Zacharias as vice-chancellor and M.M. Sangodkar as registrar.

Statutory Bodies of the Goa University: Statutory bodies of the university are as follows:

The Court: The Court has a membership of 40 and its

constitution shall be as under: (i) Vice Chancellor as chairman (ii) Five deans of faculties (iii) Five professors of university teaching departments (iv) Five principals of affiliated colleges (v) Three teachers (other than deans and professors) of the University teaching departments (vi) Eight teachers of affiliated colleges (vii) Two representatives of the managements of the non-government affiliated colleges (viii) The chairman of the University Students Council (ix) Four eminent educationists, scholars, specialists or administrators (x) One representative of the Scheduled Castes/ Scheduled Tribes and one representative of Other Backward Communities (xi) Two women representatives of Goa (xii) A representative of the non-teaching staff of the University (xiii) Registrar of the University as Member-Secretary. The term of the court will be of four years.

The Executive Council: The Executive Council has a membership of 13 and its constitution shall be as under: (i) Vice-Chancellor as chairman (ii) Two deans of faculties members (iii) One principal of an affiliated college (iv) One professor (other than deans) of the University teaching departments (v) Five eminent educationists, scholars, specialists or administrators (vi) Two nominees of the state (vii) Registrar as Member-Secretary. The term of the Executive Council is of four years

The Academic Council: Dr. Peter R de Souza, till recently head of the Goa University's Political Science Department, before a Gandhi silhouette

The Academic Council has a membership of 40 and its constitution shall be as under: (i) Vice-Chancellor as chairman (ii) All the deans of the faculties of the University (ten) (iii) Five University professors (iv) Five principals of the affiliated colleges (v) Five teachers of the University departments (vi) Five teachers of the affiliated colleges (vii) The Director of N.I.O (viii) Chairman, Goa Board of Secondary & Higher Secondary Education (ix) Three eminent educationists or scholars (x) Librarian (xi) Registrar as Member-Secretary. The term of the Academic Council is of four years.

Planning Board: The Planning Board comprises eight members and its constitution shall be as under: (i) Vice-Chancellor as chairman (ii) Vice-Chancellor of any University (iii) One member of the Executive Council (iv) One member of the Academic Council (v) One dean of faculty (vi) One eminent educationist (vii) One representative of the University Grants Commission (viii) The Registrar as ex-officio Member-Secretary. (Amended by EC on 25/11/94 in view of provision contained in clause 2 of Statute 40.)

The term of office of the members other than the Vice-Chancellor and the Registrar is of four years and they shall be eligible for re-nomination.

Finance Committee: The Finance Committee of the University consists of the following eight members: (i) Vice-Chancellor as chairman (ii) Registrar (iii) Secretary to Government of Goa in-charge of University Education (iv) Secretary to Government of Goa in-charge of the Finance (v) One nominee of the E.C. from its own members (vi) Dean of the Faculty of Commerce (vii) One nominee of the Visitor (viii) The finance Officer as Member-Secretary. The Visitor nominates a person not connected with the University on the Finance Committee. The Executive Council nominates one of its members on the Finance Committee The term of all the members of the Finance Committee other than the Vice-Chancellor and Ex-Officio Members shall be of four year.

GOMANTAK MARATHI ACADEMY

Gomantak Marathi Academy sometimes called *Goa Marathi Academy* is a pro-Marathi school established on 1987. The GMA has formed more than 56 centres working for the development of language and culture of Marathi population in Goa. The Academy has been using their services to mobilise support for various activities like literature, culture, art, drama, etc. GMA has The worked hard to make Marathi, an official language in Goa and terms Konkani as dialect of Marathi. GMA has significantly contributed for defending Marathi and its people in Goa.

MES COLLEGE

MES - Mormugao Education Society is a college in Zuarinagar, just alongside the port city of Vasco da Gama in Goa, western India.

MES offers Higher Secondary Education in Science, Commerce, Arts and Vocational courses. It also offers post graduation courses in Arts, Commerce, BCA, and BBA. It is one of the younger colleges of Goa, but caters to students from a wide area around the Mormugao taluka.

It is an affiliated college of the Goa University, which says that the college's acting principal is Dinesh A. Kamat.

This college's Dr. Maria do Ceu Rodrigues has been involved with the Lokniti/CSDS and has been the Goa state coordinator for the National Election Study 2004 apart from being engaged with a UGC Project on "Fishing in Goa, Economic, Social and Political Aspects".

THE PARVATIBAI CHOWGULE COLLEGE

Smt Parvatibai Chowgule College is a college based in the south Goa city of Margao, on the west coast of India.

Courses Offered: It offers courses in the Bachelor of Arts, Bachelor of Science, Masters of Arts (Geography), Masters of Science (Information Science) streams and Post-Graduate Diploma in Computer Application.

As the main college for Arts and Science education in South Goa since the early 'sixties, it has been home to a number of prominent alumni. Its present principal is A S Kanade. It is the only college in Margao, Goa that does not impose the wearing of a uniform on its students.

TOLANI MARITIME INSTITUTE

Tolani Maritime Institute is a maritime college in Pune, India which was established in 1998. It has about 1,500 students in its campus based and distance learning programmes. It was set up by the The Tolani Group, a ship-owning and ship management company, which perceived a need for India to produce increasing numbers of well-educated marine officers. TMI and its courses are approved by the Directorate General of Shipping (DGS), which is responsible for maritime administration and for overseeing maritime education and training in India. TMI degree programmes are conducted in collaboration with the Birla Institute of Technology and Science (BITS), Pilani. TMI is a member of the Association of Maritime Education and Training Institutions in Asia-Pacific (AMETIAP). The goal of AMETIAP, which has over 85 members, consisting of maritime training institutions throughout the Asia-Pacific region, is to foster cross-border cooperation and to improve the quality of maritime training and education.

SCHOOL EDUCATION

The quality of state-run schools and the low level of corruption has added to the betterment of education in Goa. There is not much demand for private schools in Goa as people are quite happy with the performance of the government schools at all levels. There are approximately 2,153 schools in Goa which includes primary schools, middle schools, secondary schools and higher secondary schools.

2011 Census

State/District	Literacy rate
Goa	88.7%
North Goa	89.57%
South Goa	87.59%

Most of the schools in Goa are affiliated with the state board of education. However, one can also come across schools affiliated to the CBSE and ICSE board. English is the main medium of instruction at the schools in Goa. Konkani and Portuguese are also taught in several schools of the state. Infant Jesus High School, Kendriya Vidyalaya No.1, Anjuman High School, Bal Bharati Vidya Mandir High School, Don Bosco School, Holy Cross

High School, Guardian Angel High School are some of the renowned schools in Goa. Goa is multidimensional hub for education.

Higher education

Goa University is the premier center of higher studies in the state and most of the colleges are affiliated to it. One can also come across medical and engineering colleges in Goa. There exists both private and government engineering colleges in the state. BITS Pilani — Goa is also a renowned institute which grants admission to the students on the basis of their performance in the all India aptitude test conducted by the institute. Some of the colleges in Goa offer courses in arts, commerce, science, law, architecture, dentistry, marine engineering, hotel management, fisheries and pharmacy. The National Centre for Antacrtic and Ocean Research (NCAOR),Vasco-da-Gama and the National Institute of Oceanography (NIO), Dona Paula are scientific oceanographic laboratories located in Goa, offering training and opportunities for further studies and research in affiliation with universities like Goa University etc. Goa Institute of Management established in the year 1993 is a famous B-School of the region. Students interested in the study of the Portuguese language can pursue an undergraduate and a postgraduate degree in Portuguese from Goa University or inculcate conversational skills through short term certificate course at various centres run by the Instituto Camões and the Indo-Portuguese Society.

Bibliography

Ardley, Bridget.*India.*Englewood Cliffs, N.J.: Silver Burdett Press, 1989.

Atri, Ajit : *Gandhi's View of Legal Justice*, New Delhi, Deep and Deep Pub., 2007.

Barker, Amanda.*India.*Crystal Lake, Ill.: Ribgy Interactive Library, 1996.

Burman, J.J. Roy: *Gujarat Unknown : Hindu-Muslim Syncretism and Humanistic Forays*, Mittal, Delhi, 2005.

Coleman, James S. and Rosberg jr., Carl G.: *Political Parties and National Integration in Tropical Africa*, Berkely, 1964.

Cumming, David.*India.*New York: Bookwright, 1991.

Das, Prodeepta.*Inside India.*New York: F. Watts, 1990.

Dolcini, Donatella.*India in the Islamic Era and Southeast Asia (8th to 19th century).*Austin, Tex.: Raintree Steck-Vaughn, 1997.

Gaur, Sanjay: *Narendra Modi : Change We can Believe In*, Yking Books, Delhi, 2014.

Ghoshal, U. N.: A *History of Indian Political Ideas.* London, 1966.

Gupta, L.C., M.C. Gupta, Anil Sinha and Vinod K. Sharma *Gujarat Earthquake 26 January, 2001*, Indian Institute of Public Administration, Delhi, 2002.

Jack Kemp: *A Monetary Agenda for the World Economy,* Boston, Quantum, 1984.

Jain S.C. : *New Trends in Rural Marketing*, RBSA Pub, Delhi, 2011.

Jeffrey D. Jones: *Handbook of Business Valuation*, New York: Wiley, 1992.

Judith, E.: *The Sexual Exploitation of Panchayati Raj*, Cambridge, Polity Press, 1986.

Kalman, Bobbie.*India: The Culture.*Toronto: Crabtree Publishing Co., 1990.

Kalman, Bobbie.*India: The Culture.*Toronto: Crabtree Publishing Co., 1990.

Kamble, N. D.: *Deprived Castes and their Struggle for Equality*, Ashish Publishing House, New Delhi, 1983.

Kelly, F. P.: *Charging and Accounting for Bursty Connections*, Massachusetts, MIT Press, 1997.

Kenneth L.: *Ahmedabad: A Study in Indian Urban History*, Berkeley, University of California Press, 1968.

Kieve, L.: *Urban Land Economics*, London, MacMillan Press, 1977.

Loomes, G.: *Current Issues in Microeconomics*, New York: St. Martin's Press, 1989.

Martin, Gerald D.: *Determining Economic Damages*, Santa Ana, CA: James Publishing, 1995.

Mazumder, Sukhendu : *Politico-Economic Ideas of Mahatma Gandhi : Their Relevance in the Present Day*, New Delhi, Concept Pub., 2004.

Mehta, Nalin and Mona G. Mehta: *Gujarat Beyond Gandhi: Identity, Conflict and Society*, Routledge, Delhi, 2011.

Mehta, Nalin and Mona G. Mehta: *Gujarat Beyond Gandhi: Identity, Conflict and Society*, Routledge, Delhi, 2011.

Morris-Jones, W.H.: *The Government and Politics of India*, London, Hutchinson, 1971.

Pandian, Jacob.*The Making of India and Indian Traditions.*Englewood Cliffs, N.J.: Prentice Hall, 1995.

Rao, Ramesh N. and Koenraad Elst: *Gujarat After Godhra: Real Violence Selective Outrage*, Har-anand Publications, Delhi, 2010.

Index

❑❑❑

www.ingramcontent.com/pod-product-compliance
Ingram Content Group UK Ltd.
Pitfield, Milton Keynes, MK11 3LW, UK
UKHW042016290726
14061UKWH00001BB/21

9 789388 318891